ECONOMICS

in Plain English

**DEFINITIONS.
EXAMPLES.
USES.**

ECONOMICS

in Plain English

DEFINITIONS.
EXAMPLES.
USES.

David A. Mayer

Adams Media
New York Amsterdam/Antwerp London Toronto Sydney/Melbourne New Delhi

Adams Media
An Imprint of Simon & Schuster, LLC
100 Technology Center Drive
Stoughton, MA 02072

First Adams Media hardcover edition
May 2025

ADAMS MEDIA and colophon are registered trademarks of Simon & Schuster, LLC.

Simon & Schuster strongly believes in freedom of expression and stands against censorship in all its forms. For more information, visit BooksBelong.com.

For information about special discounts for bulk purchases, please contact Simon & Schuster Special Sales at 1-866-506-1949 or business@simonandschuster.com.

The Simon & Schuster Speakers Bureau can bring authors to your live event. For more information or to book an event, contact the Simon & Schuster Speakers Bureau at 1-866-248-3049 or visit our website at www.simonspeakers.com.

Interior design by Colleen Cunningham

Interior images © Adobe Stock/musmellow, Tsvetina

Manufactured in the United States of America

1 2025

Library of Congress Cataloging-in-Publication Data
Names: Mayer, David A., 1969– author.
Title: Economics in plain English / David A. Mayer.
Description: First Adams Media hardcover edition. | Stoughton, Massachusetts: Adams Media, [2025] | Series: Financial literacy guide series
Identifiers: LCCN 2024055872 | ISBN 9781507223901 (hc) | ISBN 9781507223918 (ebook)
Classification: LCC HB171 .M46123 2025 | DDC 330--dc23/eng/20241121
LC record available at https://lccn.loc.gov/2024055872

ISBN 978-1-5072-2390-1
ISBN 978-1-5072-2391-8 (ebook)

Contents

Introduction

Understanding what is happening with the economy can be hard—and confusing. To truly follow the economy, you need to both understand and use the terms that describe it. For example, you need to know when it is appropriate to utilize a loan, how a union affects wages and other factors at an organization (in case you find yourself a part of one), and how unemployment benefits help you stay afloat until you find a new job. Learning about economic terms and the economic way of thinking will help advance your financial goals, impact how you manage your money, and shed light on how other people, businesses, and governments make economic decisions. And sometimes what you need the most is to have terms explained plainly.

That's where *Economics in Plain English* comes in. Here you'll find more than 300 glossary terms that define and clarify any economics language you'll come across. After all, whether you're a seasoned pro or someone just looking to improve your economic literacy, sometimes an easy-to-understand explanation to guide or teach you is exactly what's needed—which is why each glossary term is so simple to follow. First, each term is quickly summarized. Then, the "What it is" section provides a clear definition. Next, the "How it works" section further contextualizes and explains the concept. Finally, the "How it is used" example provides the term within an everyday sentence.

Throughout the book, you'll find the glossary terms grouped into common economic categories that will help you understand each term in context. For example:

- **Chapter 2: Costs and Production** includes terms such as *diminishing returns, economy of scale,* and *marginal revenue.*
- **Chapter 3: Degrees of Competition** provides definitions for *game theory, monopoly,* and *oligopoly.*
- **Chapter 5: Resource Markets** has lingo like *collective bargaining, efficiency wage,* and *monopsony.*
- **Chapter 8: Policy Economics** focuses on topics like *austerity, debt monetization,* and *monetary policy.*
- **Chapter 10: Growth and Inequality** gives you context for terms such as *capital deepening, labor productivity,* and *tax incidence.*
- And there are plenty more!

Ultimately, whether you need a refresher on monopolies or want to know what terms to use when discussing the effects of the economy on your personal finances, *Economics in Plain English* will help you understand the complexities of the economy and more. Using this book, you can confidently take an active role in working, shopping, investing, paying taxes, and beyond. The clear information in this book will help you navigate the economy—and how it impacts your personal finances—easily and successfully.

CHAPTER 1

The Basics

Economics has a unique vocabulary, setting it apart from any other academic or professional field. Because people all over the world make choices in line with their wants, needs, and goals, many terms have developed throughout the years. Economists and philosophers alike have answered questions through years of study, including: What are the basics of economics? How does economics function on a micro and macro level?

The terms in this chapter describe economic basics by defining how people behave and adapt to the presence of universal scarcity. From studying incentives people face, we gain a better understanding of the systems they create to allocate goods, services, and the factors of production to maximize their utility.

allocation

determination of who gets items or services of value

What it is: the share of resources that a person or institution gets in an economy

How it works: People and institutions often have to compete to get much needed, sometimes scarce resources, goods, and services. Depending on a society's economic type, allocation is determined by tradition, government, markets, or a combination of these.

In traditional economies, allocation is determined by gender roles, age, or family. In command economies, allocation is determined by governmental central planners. In market economies, allocation is determined by competition between producers and consumers, each pursuing their own self-interest. Allocation in most modern economies is determined by a combination of central planning and markets.

How it is used: During World War II, the US government controlled the economy, using community ration boards to determine the **allocation** of goods and services.

arbitrage

buying low and selling high

What it is: buying something at a low price in one setting and charging more in another to make a profit

How it works: Arbitrage is when individuals and businesses can profit when they acquire something for a cheap price in one location and then resell elsewhere for more money. The opportunity of profiting incentivizes individuals and businesses to sell goods and services in a variety of locations to satisfy people's wants or needs. For example, coffee grown in tropical places is both relatively cheap and plentiful. Coffee businesses make a profit by growing or buying the coffee in the tropics and then selling it at a higher price to consumers abroad. Competition among sellers, transportation costs, regulations, taxes, or risk may limit businesses' profit, hindering arbitrage.

How it is used: Arbitrage opportunities encourage businesses to seek new markets.

barter
trading without using money

What it is: trading a good or service in exchange for something else

How it works: Without using money, people can trade a good or service they provide so they can get something they need or want. For example, a local dentist in need of accounting services may offer to trade dental care for an accountant's time. Barter depends upon people wanting something from one another. If the accountant, for example, does not require dental services, then the dentist would have to search for an accountant who needs their teeth cleaned.

How it is used: Before the invention of money, people used to **barter** to get what they wanted.

black market
illegal buying and selling

What it is: a market in goods or services hidden from the government

How it works: Governments may regulate, tax, or prohibit the buying and selling of different goods or services. If there is sufficient demand, then a black market may develop where the good or service is bought and sold without the government's approval or intervention. Black markets develop when goods and services are illegal, there are price controls on them, or people are trying to avoid paying taxes for them. The presence of black markets often undermine governments' attempts to regulate, tax, or prohibit certain goods and services.

How it is used: During the early 1970s, a **black market** for certain foods developed to avoid the government's price controls.

capital
things made to make other things

What it is: equipment and the places needed to produce other goods or services

How it works: Capital (or physical capital) is one of the four factors of production in the economy. People need tools, machines, equipment, factories, and buildings to produce all the goods and services in the economy. Over time, the creation of capital allows for a growing economy. As the amount of capital in an economy grows, the productive capacity of workers in that economy expands and allows for further future production. Capital results from people investing their savings rather than spending the money elsewhere. Without capital, a society cannot produce goods.

How it is used: Linda invested in **capital**—including a printing press—when she started her independent newspaper.

capitalism
private ownership of capital

What it is: a system in which capital is private property rather than being owned by the government

How it works: People can buy capital from other businesses and either individually, jointly, or by hiring workers can operate that capital to produce goods and services. The owner(s) of the capital, called capitalist(s), is (are) entitled to a share of the profits from the sale of their goods and services. The profits tend to be greater than the wage that capitalist would have earned if otherwise employed. Capitalistic economies often offer a greater variety of goods and services and have higher standards of living than other economies.

How it is used: After the collapse of communism in Eastern Europe, many government-owned businesses were sold to private citizens as the countries started to practice **capitalism**.

ceteris paribus
other things staying constant

What it is: an assumption in economics used when trying to understand the relationship between two variables

How it works: In an economy, many variables are constantly changing. To better understand how two variables might relate to each other, economists use the ceteris paribus assumption, or that all other outside variables stay the same when measuring the two specific variables, to simplify and explain the effect of one variable on another. By holding all other factors constant, economists can better explain the cause-and-effect relationship between any two specific variables. However, unlike a science experiment with built-in controls, economists must analyze data from the real world to understand economic relationships. Forgoing experimental control variables, economists study historical data and make repeated observations through different periods. Then, economists can more easily determine the causal relationships between economic variables.

How it is used: An increase in the real interest rate results in less private investment **ceteris paribus**.

command economy
complete government control over the entire economy

What it is: an economic system in which all production and allocation of resources, goods, and services is determined by the government

How it works: In a command economy, the government directs all aspects of production, distribution, and allocation of items and services. All decision-making regarding economic capital, labor, and natural resources is left to central planners; these planners determine what gets produced, how it's produced, and who gets the product. These economies can direct resources wherever the government desires, which may not align with the wants and needs of individuals in the economy. So, most people in command economies can't choose how their lives are spent, what they do for work, or where they live.

How it is used: People in North Korea have little economic freedom because they live in a **command economy**.

complementary good/service
a good or service consumed alongside another good or service

What it is: goods or services that are often consumed or utilized together

How it works: When the price of food at restaurants increases, there will be less demand for drinks at those restaurants because fewer consumers will buy meals out. When the price of food decreases, the demand for drinks increases because the consumer's dollar is stronger. Economists determine if goods are complementary by calculating their cross-price elasticity of demand. This is calculated by taking the rate of change in the quantity of a demanded good divided by the rate of change in the price of another good. If the result is negative, then the goods are complementary.

How it is used: An economist determined that lift tickets and ski rentals were **complementary goods**, advising the ski rental and lift ticket businesses to work together.

consumer surplus

the extra benefit of buying a good or service at a lower-than-expected price

What it is: the total monetary benefit of paying less than what a person would have willingly paid for a good or service; the difference between the highest price the consumers would willingly pay and the market price

How it works: Consumer surplus is calculated by adding up all the individual benefits for each buyer in a market who would have willingly paid more for the good or service than the market price. Consumer surplus is at its greatest in markets with perfect competition. If producers can charge each customer a different price, then consumer surplus is eliminated, so government does not allow this.

How it is used: I would have paid $25 for the ticket, but it was only $10 online; this meant I had $15 of **consumer surplus**.

demand

ability and willingness to buy

What it is: when there are consumers in a market who are willing and able to purchase a good or service

How it works: The price of a good or service affects how much it is demanded. When things are more expensive, people are less likely to buy them because it both takes too much of their income and there are likely cheaper alternatives. When things are cheaper, people can afford to buy more of the good or service and won't look for substitutes. Together these show that as the price of something changes, the amount demanded changes in the opposite direction. Changes in the number of consumers, consumers' incomes, prices of related goods, tastes and preferences, and expectations for the future all impact demand, altering the original price.

How it is used: Demand for electric vehicles has increased in recent years as gasoline prices have risen.

diminishing marginal utility

satisfaction shrinks with each additional unit of consumption

What it is: as people consume more of a good or service, each additional unit used provides less benefit than the previous one

How it works: Diminishing marginal utility is the concept that continuing to buy more of the same thing provides less and less benefit. For example, the purchase of a sandwich provides the consumer with the food they require for the afternoon, but the purchase of a second, third, or fourth sandwich provides increasingly less benefit than the first one because the consumer may already be full. Because of diminishing marginal utility, consumers will only buy additional units of a good or service if the price is lower than what they paid for the first unit consumed.

How it is used: The average price per slice of pizza is cheaper if you buy a whole pizza rather than buying it by the slice because of **diminishing marginal utility**.

economics

the subject of how people deal with scarcity

What it is: a social science that studies the choices people make to deal with not having enough of what they need or want

How it works: Economics is a diverse discipline that looks at everything people do to manage sometimes difficult-to-attain wants and needs in the face of scarce resources. Economics studies how people produce, distribute, and allocate goods, services, and resources; it is both influenced by and influences other social sciences such as sociology, psychology, and political science. However, economics tends to be more math-intensive than other social sciences because it involves measuring and calculating different data. People who study economics are called economists.

How it is used: To better understand the effects of proposed taxes on people's behavior, the president called his chief **economic** advisor.

economy

how people get what they want or need

What it is: a system that allocates scarce resources to produce and distribute goods and services to people

How it works: An economy is made up of households, businesses, governments, and countries all over the world. Each of these exchange with each other to meet their wants and needs. The decisions of what, how, and for whom to produce depend upon the economic type of the country. An economy is measured using GDP (gross domestic product), and its overall health is determined by the size of its labor force, amount of capital present, unemployment rate, inflation rate, and more.

How it is used: In 2023, the US **economy** produced about $27 trillion of goods and services, making it the leading economic force in the world.

elasticity of demand

sensitivity of demand to price changes in the market

What it is: a math ratio that shows how the rate of change in the amount demanded is affected by the rate of change in price

How it works: Elasticity of demand depends upon time, proportion of income, availability of substitutes, necessity, durability, and other factors. When a change in price results in a larger change in the amount demanded, then demand is elastic. When a change in price results in little change in the amount demanded, then demand is inelastic. Elasticity of demand is important for businesses because it helps them decide if they should charge a higher or lower price to make money. When demand is elastic, they increase their earnings by charging a lower price, but when demand is inelastic, they increase money earned by charging a higher price.

How it is used: A gas station can increase the price it charges for gasoline right before a busy travel day because drivers' **elasticity of demand** for fuel will be relatively inelastic.

elasticity of supply
sensitivity of supply to price changes in the market

What it is: a math ratio that shows how the rate of change in the amount supplied is affected by the rate of change in price

How it works: Elasticity of supply mainly depends upon the amount of time it takes to produce a good or service. When it takes a long time to produce something, then it has an inelastic supply. However, when something can be produced quickly, then it has an elastic supply. Elasticity of supply is important because when there is a sudden increase in demand for a good with inelastic supply, then consumers will have to pay a higher price than if the good had elastic supply.

How it is used: The **elasticity of supply** for fine violins is inelastic because it takes a long time to produce each one.

entrepreneurship
risk-taking in search of profits

What it is: a person's (or people's) ability to take risks by starting new businesses in search of profits

How it works: Entrepreneurship is one of the four factors of production in economics; it's unique because only entrepreneurship makes use of the other three (land, labor, and capital) to form a new business. Individuals with this skill (called entrepreneurs) are willing to risk not earning wages working under someone else for the chance to make more money from their profits. Whether or not entrepreneurship is allowed or encouraged depends upon the type of economy a country has. In command economies, entrepreneurship is discouraged or prohibited, but in market economies, it is encouraged.

How it is used: Parents often encourage children to practice **entrepreneurship** by helping them open a lemonade stand on a hot day.

equilibrium

when the amount supplied and demanded is equal

What it is: a condition in a market where the price results in the same amount of a good or service being both supplied and demanded

How it works: Equilibrium clears the market where there is neither too much nor not enough of a good or service. Markets reach equilibrium after changes in supply or demand, generally when buyers and producers of goods are competing amongst themselves. When a market has a surplus (too much of a good or service), producers lower the accepted price, and consumers then buy more until the market is in equilibrium. When a market has a shortage, consumers compete by offering more money to get the good or service, and producers then sell more until the market again reaches equilibrium.

How it is used: The commercial real estate market is not in **equilibrium** because there is currently a surplus of office space in cities, meaning office rents should decrease.

inferior good

decreased income increases demand for the good

What it is: goods people are more likely to buy if they have lower income

How it works: Determining whether a good is inferior or not is based on a calculation. Goods are inferior if the income elasticity of demand for the good is negative. Income elasticity of demand is calculated by dividing the rate of change in the amount of a good demanded by the rate of change in consumers' income. For example, as income increases, economists calculate that consumers are less likely to consume instant ramen noodles. These people are more likely to consume ramen from a restaurant. So, the income elasticity of demand for the instant noodles is negative. Inferior goods are the opposite of normal goods (the restaurant ramen in the example just mentioned), which have a positive income elasticity of demand.

How it is used: During the Great Depression, demand for **inferior goods** like hot dogs increased while demand for normal goods like steaks decreased because people were making less money.

interest

the cost of borrowing

What it is: the amount of money a borrower pays a lender or saver to use their money

How it works: When consumers or businesses want to borrow money, they must pay the lender more than just the amount borrowed. These borrowers must also pay the lender interest, because the lender is forgoing the use of the money. Interest payments on debt are a cost to borrowers but income to savers and lenders. The amount of interest people pay or earn is determined by the interest rate. As interest rates increase, people are more likely to save and less likely to borrow, but when interest rates decrease, people are less likely to save and more likely to borrow.

How it is used: As the US government's debt increases, so do its **interest** payments; this leaves less money for other types of spending in the government's budget.

labor

human resources

What it is: the combined skills, abilities, and effort of people willing and able to work

How it works: Labor, or human workers, is one of the four factors of production in an economy and, besides entrepreneurship, is the only factor made up of people. Labor performs work in the economy in exchange for wages from their employer. The amount of labor employed in an economy (given a fixed amount of capital) determines the economy's real output.

Labor is often divided into several classifications based on the nature of the work performed. Labor is considered *unskilled* when the work is primarily physical and can be done with little or no training. Examples of unskilled labor include cashiers, waitstaff, and assembly-line factory workers. Labor is considered *skilled* when the work is primarily physical but requires significant training. Examples of skilled labor include electricians, plumbers, mechanics, HVAC technicians, and paid athletes. Labor is considered *professional* when the work is primarily mental and requires significant training.

Examples of professional labor include accountants, attorneys, doctors, programmers, teachers, and managers.

How it is used: During an economic expansion, businesses compete by offering higher wages to attract **labor** to come work for them.

land

natural resources

What it is: all natural resources used by businesses to produce goods and services

How it works: Unlike the other three factors of production (labor, capital, and entrepreneurship), land is the most limited; no more of it can be produced. Natural resources that are nonrenewable, like fossil fuels, limit the ability of an economy to produce indefinitely and act as a constraint on an economy's long-term growth. As natural resources become more and more scarce, their increased cost, or rent, forces businesses to operate more efficiently to profit. This in turn, allows some natural resources to remain for future production.

How it is used: To expand the future availability of **land** in the economy, entrepreneurs and scientists are now conducting research on how to extract minerals from asteroids, moons, and even other planets.

macroeconomics

study of how entire societies manage to deal with scarcity

What it is: this branch of economics focuses on how societies deal with scarcity while maintaining economic stability

How it works: The field of macroeconomics (one of two major branches of economics) gained importance during and after the economic impact of the Great Depression in the 1930s. As a result of that monetary tragedy, economists were forced to reconsider their understanding of how the economy worked. They began building a set of theories to explain how the Depression happened and what to do to avoid future depressions. Macroeconomics can be further divided into different areas of study such as economic measurement, macroeconomic modeling, money and banking, stabilization policy, and international economics.

How it is used: Members of the president's Council of Economic Advisers often have advanced college degrees in **macroeconomics** because they make policies that affect the entire economy.

marginal benefit or marginal utility
benefit of utilizing an additional item

What it is: the positive effect of consuming an additional unit of a good or service

How it works: Economists use marginal analysis where they compare the additional benefit of buying something to its cost to understand if consumers should continue utilizing the goods or services. The benefit a person receives from an additional unit of a good or service is called its marginal benefit or marginal utility. If the marginal benefit exceeds the cost of consuming an additional unit of a good or service, then the consumer should continue partaking in the good or service. By continuing to consume up to the point where the marginal benefit equals the marginal cost of consumption, customers maximize their economic well-being.

How it is used: A hungry customer decided to buy an additional slice of pizza because the **marginal benefit** was greater than the cost of a slice.

marginal cost
cost of producing one more

What it is: the amount a producer must pay to increase production of a good or service by one unit

How it works: Economists use something called marginal analysis to understand if a company should continue making a good or service. The cost a company must pay to produce an additional unit of a good or service is called its marginal cost. If the marginal cost is less than the price the company can charge for the good or service, then the company should continue to produce. By continuing to create something up to the point where the price the company can charge equals the marginal cost, companies can maximize their economic well-being.

How it is used: A business able to charge customers $100 per pickleball paddle should continue to produce paddles up until their **marginal cost** is $100 to maximize their total profit.

market

where buyers and sellers come together to exchange

What it is: where producers and consumers exchange goods, services, and resources

How it works: A market is not necessarily a physical place, but a concept. In a market, individual sellers and buyers each pursue their own self-interest while trying to maximize their personal well-being, and they come together to satisfy their needs and wants. Instead of a government or central planner telling them what, how, or for whom to produce, producers and consumers voluntarily exchange in a market driven by their own self-interest and desire to be better off than they were before.

How it is used: Many Americans prefer to allow **markets** to allocate goods, services, and resources rather than having the government do it.

market clearing price

equilibrium price

What it is: the price that eliminates surpluses or shortages in the market

How it works: When supply is equal to demand in a market, the market has neither a surplus nor a shortage, and the price associated with this condition is called the market clearing price. It's considered market clearing because there is neither too much nor not enough of the good in the market. When surpluses and shortages occur, competition among buyers and sellers ultimately steer the market to its market clearing price. The market clearing price is considered the most efficient outcome because utility is maximized for producers and consumers at that price.

How it is used: After a sudden decrease in the supply of crude oil caused a shortage, the market adjusted to a higher **market clearing price**.

market economy

economy free of government control

What it is: an economic system in which all production and allocation of resources, goods, and services is determined by voluntary exchange between individual producers and consumers through markets

How it works: Instead of relying on government or central planners to make key economic decisions, in a market economy, individuals looking to make beneficial monetary investments voluntarily exchange with others. These investments happen in markets where they allocate goods, services, and resources. Decision-making is completely decentralized, and government does not interfere with the economy.

How it is used: Although much of the decision-making regarding production and allocation is determined by markets in the US, the government still provides public goods and services, so this country does not actually have a pure **market economy**.

microeconomics

study of people's and businesses' choices when they either produce or consume

What it is: as one of the two major branches in economics, microeconomics focuses on how individuals and businesses interact in a market, given the scarcity of resources

How it works: The field of microeconomics looks at how utility-maximizing businesses and individuals interact in product and resource markets. Microeconomics is interested in how these people and businesses make financial decisions.

Microeconomics is further divided into areas of study such as basic market analysis, the theory of the firm, degrees of competition in markets, market failures, and resource markets. As a subject, microeconomics is founded on both direct observation through experimentation as well as interpreting real-world data.

How it is used: People who are interested in a business career should take a **microeconomics** class so they can better understand the environment in which businesses operate.

mixed economy

combination of market and command economic systems

What it is: an economic system that combines elements of market economy with elements of command economy to answer key economic decisions

How it works: Most economies in the world today use markets to allocate goods, services, and resources in combination with some government control of the economy. Mixed economies are not all the same; some practice *socialism* where the government controls key industries and allows markets to exist for most consumer goods and services. Other mixed economies offer a higher degree of freedom by allowing private individuals and firms to own all businesses, while the government acts as the regulator and provider of goods and services not supplied by private firms. For example, the US has a mixed economy in which government regulates markets and provides public goods and services such as police protection, public schooling, firefighting, and roads. The markets then provide the rest of what people need or want.

How it is used: Trying to find the right balance between government control and economic freedom for individuals and firms is the main challenge facing societies with a **mixed economy**.

normal good

income and demand for the good are directly related

What it is: a good people tend to buy more of as their income increases

How it works: A good is considered normal if its income elasticity of demand is positive. This is calculated by dividing the rate of change in the amount of the good demanded by the rate of change in consumers' income. Most of the goods we consume are normal goods, not inferior goods. So as incomes rise, demand for these goods increases as well. For example, as consumers' incomes rise, so does their demand for new cars. Normal goods can be further subdivided into normal necessities and normal luxuries. Normal necessities have positive income elasticities of demand less than one, and normal luxuries have income elasticities of demand greater than or equal to one. Normal necessities include things like toothpaste and toilet paper. Normal luxuries include dining out and electric cars.

How it is used: An economist calculated that theme park tickets are a **normal good** because the income elasticity of demand was positive.

opportunity cost
what is given up to get something else

What it is: the next best alternative use of money, time, or scarce resources

How it works: People face many choices of how to best use the money, time, or scarce resources they possess. Once they decide to use one of these for a particular purpose, they lose the ability to use it for something else. For example, a person may face the decision of going in early for work or sleeping later. Whichever decision is made, the opportunity cost is what was sacrificed. If the person decides to sleep late, then the opportunity cost of the decision was the income they could have earned by showing up early for work. If, however, they decide to show up early for work, the opportunity cost is the extra sleep they could have enjoyed.

How it is used: An economics student determined that, for them, the **opportunity cost** of going to college for 4 years is the money they could have earned by working full-time.

price
money paid per unit

What it is: the amount a consumer pays for a single unit of a good or service

How it works: In a market, price is determined by the competing forces of supply and demand. In a purely competitive market, no single person or business sets the price, but it is instead determined by the market itself. Other times, the price of a good or service might be determined by a dominant business or even by government regulation, and yet at other times the price might be determined by a dominant consumer. Prices can be expressed in units of money, but they can also be expressed as interest or exchange rates. In the absence of money, prices may even be expressed as some amount of another good offered in exchange. Prices perform an important function in markets because they ration who gets what based on their willingness and ability to pay.

How it is used: Yesterday the **price** of gasoline was $3.00 per gallon.

price ceiling

maximum legal price

What it is: a highest possible price for a good, service, or resource set by the government

How it works: Sometimes governments decide that the market price for a necessity is too high for the average consumer, so they set a price ceiling so these consumers can afford it. Price ceilings are considered effective if the price ceiling is less than the market price. If effective, price ceilings may result in shortages of the good because, at the ceiling, the amount demanded may be greater than the amount supplied. When these shortages occur, governments must find other ways to ration the good. Economists generally agree that price ceilings are problematic.

How it is used: A city council determined that apartment rent was too high for some low-income households, so they imposed an effective **price ceiling** on rent.

price floor

lowest possible legal price

What it is: a minimum price for a good, service, or resource set by the government

How it works: Sometimes governments decide that the market price for a good or resource is too low, so they set a price floor, making the item more expensive. Price floors are considered effective if the price floor is greater than the market price. If effective, price floors may result in surpluses because, at the floor, the amount demanded may be less than the amount supplied. When these surpluses occur, governments must find ways to pay for the extras. Economists generally agree that price floors are problematic. For example, setting a per bushel price floor on wheat ensures that farmers who manage to sell their wheat will earn a higher price, but because the higher price incentivizes farmers to produce more wheat, government needs to figure out how to pay farmers for any unsold wheat.

How it is used: In many large urban areas, the federal minimum wage is not an effective **price floor** because market wages are higher than the federal minimum wage.

producer surplus

the benefit of selling a good or service at a higher-than-expected price

What it is: the difference between the market price and the price at which a business would willingly sell their goods

How it works: This is the total monetary benefit of earning a price higher than what producers would have willingly accepted for a good or service, or the difference between the lowest price the producers would willingly accept and the market price. Producer surplus is calculated by totaling the individual benefit for each producer in a market who would have happily accepted less for the good or service than what the market price is set as. Producer surplus is maximized in markets where producers can charge each customer the maximum price each customer would willingly pay. This is called perfect price discrimination, and it violates federal law.

How it is used: I would have sold the used car for $10,000, but when I went to sell it, I was offered $12,000; that's $2,000 of **producer surplus**.

production possibilities curve

simple model of an economy

What it is: a basic model of an economy that illustrates its ability to produce two goods, given a fixed number of resources and technology

How it works: If an economy faces scarce resources and technology remains the same, the economy can produce a finite combination of two goods called trade-offs. All the combinations, which also use up all the resources, define the production possibilities curve (also known as the production possibilities frontier). The curve can either be a straight line or bowed out depending upon whether available resources are equally suited to produce either trade-off or not. If the resources are equally suited, then the production possibilities curve is a straight line and demonstrates constant opportunity cost. If, however, the resources are not equally suited, then the production possibilities curve is bowed out, which shows increasing opportunity costs. Changes in the availability of resources or technology has a direct effect on the production possibilities curve and causes it to shift.

How it is used: An economics professor used a diagram of the **production possibilities curve** to illustrate how an economy can grow over time.

profit

payment to entrepreneurs

What it is: when the amount of money coming in is greater than the amount of money going out for a business

How it works: Whereas most people work for someone else and earn a wage for their labor, entrepreneurs start new businesses in search of payment greater than the wage they could have earned working for someone else—they seek profit. The ability to make a profit incentivizes the entrepreneur to direct land, labor, and capital to provide new or improved goods and services to the market. This profit-seeking behavior is one of the forces that helps markets function, ultimately allocating goods and services in the economy. Profit-making relies on private ownership of land and capital and is a key attribute of market economies. Profit is one of the four factor payments along with rent, wages, and interest.

How it is used: Dissatisfied with her current wage, Aria started a new business so she could earn a **profit**.

rent

payment to landowners

What it is: when people in an economy want or need land, or natural resources, they must pay the owner money

How it works: In an economy with private property, land is owned by private individuals. These people can command a payment for the use of their land. The payment of rent allows the buyer or renter to use the associated natural resources from land for some productive purpose. Rent is one of the four factor payments along with wages, interest, and profits. Collecting rent incentivizes people to own land.

How it is used: Owners of land often have mineral rights that allow them to charge an economic **rent** to firms who extract crude oil.

scarcity

not enough

What it is: the universal condition that exists because peoples' wants and needs are greater than the available resources to satisfy them

How it works: Scarcity describes the phenomenon of people lacking the ability to have everything they want or need. Resources are not unlimited. There is only so much land, labor, capital, and entrepreneurship in any given economy. Scarcity forces people to make choices about the use of these factors of production. As a matter of fact, the whole point of economics is understanding how people and societies make decisions when faced with scarcity.

How it is used: It's nice to think that if every person shared everything equally, then everyone would be satisfied, but this ignores **scarcity**.

shortage

quantity demanded greater than quantity supplied

What it is: when the quantity demanded in a market is greater than the quantity supplied

How it works: Whenever there is a decrease in supply or increase in demand for a good or service, a shortage exists until the price increases. The shortage is usually a temporary phenomenon if the market adjusts quickly, but a shortage can persist if the price is suppressed with a price ceiling. Shortages are resolved when buyers compete by offering a higher price for the good or service and sellers then offer more of it for sale until the market clears at a new higher price. Sometimes shortages can be resolved by rationing (limiting the quantity of) a good or service that consumers can purchase.

How it is used: News of an approaching hurricane threatened to cause a **shortage** of bottled water at the local grocery store, so the store decided to limit customers to 2 gallons per household.

socialism

government ownership of capital

What it is: a system in which capital is owned by the government rather than being private property

How it works: Government ownership of capital in socialism means that government officials make the decisions on how capital is used in producing goods and services in the economy. Any profits earned belong to the government and fund its ongoing operations.

Socialism varies from country to country. In some countries, only the capital in key industries is owned by the government, while private ownership of capital exists in industries that mainly produce consumer goods. Some countries practice democratic socialism where elected representatives accountable to voters help determine how capital is used in an economy. Other countries practice authoritarian socialism where government makes the decisions on how capital is used without being accountable to its citizens.

How it is used: France practices a form of **socialism** where the government is in charge of certain industries like healthcare while businesses provide common consumer goods.

substitute good/service

item or act used in place of another

What it is: a thing or action that replaces a similar thing or action

How it works: A substitute good or service is something you can easily replace with something else, like Uber and Lyft. When the price of a good increases, demand for its substitute increases and vice versa. For example, if the price of an Uber ride increases, then we might expect the demand for Lyft, a substitute service, to increase in response. Economists can tell if goods are substitutes by calculating their cross-price elasticity of demand, or the rate of change in the amount of a good demanded divided by the rate of change in the price of some other good. If the quotient is positive, then the goods are substitutes.

How it is used: An economics student confirmed that margarine and butter are **substitute goods** when they looked at comparative sales data.

supply

willingness and ability to produce

What it is: a positive relationship between price and the amount of a good or service being produced

How it works: Companies have a willingness and ability to produce goods and services for buyers. The price of a good or service is directly related to the quantity supplied. There's more of a good or service supplied at a higher price than at a lower price because producers can afford to produce additional units. At a lower price there is less of a good or service because the cost of producing a unit might be higher than the price. Changes in the number of producers, profitability, natural phenomenon, regulations, taxes, and expectations for the future will cause supply to change. Then, the quantity of a good or service supplied at each price is different than before.

How it is used: The **supply** of electric vehicles has increased in recent years as more businesses started producing them.

surplus

more of a good or service is being offered for sale than what people are willing to buy at that price

What it is: when the quantity demanded in a market is less than the quantity supplied

How it works: Whenever there is an increase in supply or a decrease in demand for a good or service, a surplus exists until the price decreases. The surplus is usually a temporary phenomenon if the market adjusts quickly, but this surplus can persist if the price is artificially supported with a price floor. Surpluses are resolved when producers compete by accepting a lower price for the good or service and consumers then purchase more until the market clears at a new lower price.

How it is used: Faced with racks of unsold holiday sweaters, the local department store put them on sale in January to clear the **surplus**.

trade-off
alternative uses for resources

What it is: the next best use for a resource

How it works: People are always making decisions on how to best use their time, money, or resources. When ranking their choices of what to do, the top two choices become a person's trade-offs. Because of scarcity, producers face trade-offs when it comes to using the factors of production. For example, an instrument maker has a nice piece of wood that could be used as the soundboard for two trade-offs: a violin or a viola. The piece of wood cannot be used to make two instruments, so the instrument maker must choose between the one instrument or the other.

How it is used: A student woke up early on a Saturday morning and was immediately faced with the **trade-offs** of going back to sleep for another hour or finishing his homework.

traditional economy
custom, ritual, age, and gender determine who gets what

What it is: a system for deciding who gets and who produces goods based on ritual and custom rather than markets or central planning

How it works: In some societies, the decisions around what to produce, how to produce, and for whom to produce are determined by how an individual fits into the society. Men may be the hunters and warriors and women may be the caregivers and food-gatherers. The production of arrowheads might be only performed by men while tradition may dictate that only women are allowed to consume certain foods.

How it is used: A social anthropologist observed in a **traditional economy** that everyone in the society received a portion of meat according to their age and sex.

utility

satisfaction

What it is: the contentment people get from the choices they make

How it works: Utility basically translates into how happy people are after they make a decision. In economics, an important concept is that people seek to always maximize their utility. Each individual decision provides people with some level of utility, and people are best off when they have maximized that utility. The opposite of utility is disutility, or harm, which is something people seek to minimize, so people will weigh the possible utility against the disutility while making important choices. If the utility is greater than or equal to the disutility, then they go ahead with their decision.

How it is used: Economists might pessimistically argue that people perform seemingly selfless actions to maximize their **utility**.

CHAPTER 2

Costs and Production

Businesses have many hidden costs and processes that the average person may not know about. By understanding the vocabulary of how businesses, or firms, operate, and the factors that influence their decision-making, you learn more about the economy. When looking at firm size, production, costs, revenue, and profit, you can see that firms face constraints that they must account for when determining what, how, and for whom to produce.

The terms in this chapter fall into three major categories: ideal size for the firm, the relationship between the number of workers employed and output, and the inflows and outflows of money to and from firms. Understanding the ideal size of a firm includes terms like *economy of scale* or *increasing returns to scale*. Describing the relationship between the number of workers employed and the amount of output produced by firms requires understanding the terms *diminishing returns* and *production function*. Inflows and outflows are described by terms such as *marginal revenue* and *total cost*.

accounting profit
total revenue minus total explicit cost

What it is: what you get when you take a firm's complete earnings and subtract the total costs of production

How it works: Businesses produce goods and services and sell them to their customers. The total number of units sold multiplied by the price of each unit equals a firm's total revenue. From this total revenue, all the explicit costs (designing, producing, transporting, and distributing of goods or services) are subtracted. The difference between the revenue and the cost becomes the business's total profit. Businesses must then pay taxes to the government on their profits. The business can then use its after-tax profit to further expand, or it can distribute the after-tax profit to the owners of the business or some combination of the two.

How it is used: Just because a corporation has a large amount of revenue does not mean that it makes an **accounting profit**.

average costs
costs divided by a company's output

What it is: a company's costs divided by the amount of output produced by the company

How it works: Companies incur costs when they produce goods and services. Economists study costs to best understand what amount of production companies should undertake. By dividing the company's fixed, variable, and total costs by the number of units produced, economists calculate the company's different average costs. Average fixed cost is calculated by dividing total fixed cost by the quantity of units produced. Average variable cost is calculated by dividing total variable cost by the quantity of units produced. Average total cost can be calculated by either adding average fixed cost to average variable cost or by dividing total cost by the quantity of units produced. Knowing when and where average costs are at a minimum helps businesses decide their ideal level of production.

How it is used: Companies with lower **average costs** are better able to make a profit in a highly competitive market.

constant returns to scale

changing the company's size doesn't affect average total cost

What it is: when relatively small changes in the company's size do not affect the company's total average cost

How it works: As companies get bigger, they initially experience lower average costs along the way. However, if they continue to grow, the company will find that its average total cost ceases to go down. A firm that has reached that size experiences constant returns to scale and should stop expanding.

How it is used: A factory that had continually expanded with great success discovered after their last expansion that they had finally reached **constant returns to scale**.

decreasing returns

adding too many workers causes output to decrease

What it is: when a firm adds too many workers, and it becomes less productive

How it works: Let's assume a firm has a fixed amount of capital (such as tools, machines, buildings). The addition of workers initially increases the firm's output, but adding too many workers without adding additional capital results in workers sharing machines, crowded workplaces, and not enough tools to go around. Managers are supposed to make sure that the optimum number of workers is scheduled on any given day. Add too many and work suffers.

How it is used: An enterprising restaurant owner decided to increase the number of cooks in the kitchen, but he failed to consider the size of the kitchen and experienced **decreasing returns**.

decreasing returns to scale

a business can be too big

What it is: when increasing the size of the business boosts its average total cost

How it works: As firms get bigger, initially they experience lower average costs, then constant average costs, and eventually increasing average costs if they continue to expand. Average costs start to increase in relation to the size of the firm because it becomes inefficient to have factories and business centers that are larger than necessary. Productivity begins to fall while costs continue to rise, resulting in decreasing returns to scale. For example, during the Cold War, the Soviet Union boasted about having the world's largest factories. Because of the companies' sheer size, they were inefficient and costly to operate because machinery was too far apart, causing workers to waste time walking from machine to machine.

How it is used: An enterprising furniture salesman thought it might be a good idea to build the world's largest showroom, but he didn't consider **decreasing returns to scale**.

diminishing returns

each additional unit of labor contributes less to output

What it is: the point at which adding labor to a firm results in each additional worker contributing less to output than the previous worker

How it works: Assuming a firm has a fixed amount of capital (tools, machines, buildings), more workers initially boost the firm's output at an increasing rate. However, eventually more workers increase the firm's output at a diminishing rate. When a firm reaches the point of diminishing returns, it is approaching maximum output. The firm should stop adding labor when the cost of the additional worker equals the revenue earned on the next unit of output produced. In daily life, we can also apply diminishing returns. Whether it's eating, sleeping, exercising, or studying, there's a point at which an additional hour of these activities provides less benefit than the previous hour.

How it is used: A student was stressed out about an economics exam the next morning and studied for 3 hours before hitting the point of **diminishing returns**.

economic profit

total revenue minus total cost

What it is: the remaining profit after subtracting both explicit and implicit costs from a firm's total earnings

How it works: Economic profit happens when the costs of production, or explicit costs, subtracted from total money earned, are greater than they would be had the entrepreneur decided to operate in a different industry. The possible additional profits which could be earned in a different industry using the same labor and capital are the implicit cost. Economic profits are important because they attract capital and labor to an industry. When an industry lacks economic profit, capital and labor flows away from that industry and toward one with economic profit. This results in the best use of resources. Economic profit is different than accounting profit, which only accounts for explicit costs but ignores the possibility that a greater profit could be earned in a different industry. Firms want to earn and maintain economic profits, so they will engage in behavior to protect and sustain their economic profit. The presence of persistent economic profits indicates that something or someone is preventing competition.

How it is used: Electric scooters' sudden appearance in cities and the subsequent diversity of companies offering them for rent indicates that **economic profits** were being earned early on, which attracted competition.

economy of scale

sometimes bigger is better

What it is: the phenomenon of a business's growth lowering the average cost it takes to produce an item or service

How it works: As a firm gets larger, its long-run average total cost decreases as it produces more, and once it reaches a size at which long-run average total cost stops decreasing it has reached an economy of scale. Economies of scale provide a competitive advantage to larger firms because they can supply goods and services at a lower price while still making a profit. When a firm's economy of scale prevents competition in the market, government may step in to regulate or even break up the firm. It is difficult for new firms to enter a market where existing firms have an economy of scale.

How it is used: It is very difficult for new electric car manufacturers to compete in the market because so many of the existing automobile firms have **economies of scale**.

fixed cost

expenses that stay the same

What it is: prices that do not vary with the level of a firm's output

How it works: All firms incur costs when producing a good or service. Some of these costs remain constant regardless of how much the firm is producing; these are called fixed costs. Examples of fixed costs include rent, salaries, loan payments, property taxes, and some utilities. As firms increase their output, the average fixed cost (calculated by fixed costs divided by output) continuously decreases.

How it is used: One of the barriers new firms face is high **fixed costs** associated with buying capital; so instead of borrowing and making loan payments, these firms sell shares of ownership on the stock market.

increasing returns

each additional worker produces more than the previous worker

What it is: the range of production where adding labor increases a firm's output at an increasing rate

How it works: As firms add workers, the initial workers contribute continually growing amounts of output called increased returns. As long as firms experience these increasing returns, they should continue to add workers to produce more output. Eventually firms will experience diminishing returns from adding labor, but until that happens, adding workers is their right course of action. For example, restaurants operating at a point where there are still increasing returns to labor will seem understaffed and slow to customers, so the managers need to hire more waitstaff until they hit diminishing returns.

How it is used: A store manager observed that when she hired additional cashiers the store's sales increased exponentially, demonstrating **increasing returns**.

increasing returns to scale
average total cost decreases as the firm gets bigger

What it is: as firms increase in size, initially their average total cost of production decreases

How it works: As firms add tools, buy more equipment, and expand the size of their operations, they can produce more output at lower average cost, increasing their profitability. This provides the incentive for firms to further expand. These increasing returns to scale encourage continued expansion. However, continued expansion will eventually cease to lower average total cost, and at that point, the firm reaches its optimum size.

How it is used: A successful restaurateur decided to add an extra dining room and expand the kitchen at their restaurant because they calculated they would experience **increasing returns to scale**.

marginal revenue
money earned from selling an additional unit

What it is: the change in total revenue from selling an additional unit of output

How it works: Each time a firm sells a product, it earns additional revenue. If a firm is in a perfectly competitive market, or if a firm can charge each customer their maximum willing price, then the marginal revenue earned equals the price determined in the market. If, however, the firm is in a less competitive market, then the price they earn for each product sold is greater than the marginal revenue.

The reason marginal revenue is less than the price when markets are not competitive is that, to sell additional units, the firm must lower the price they charge for all the units, which results in marginal revenue decreasing at a faster rate than the price. It's important for businesses to understand their marginal revenue because they maximize their profit when they produce at a point where marginal revenue equals the cost of producing an additional unit.

How it is used: A local farmer sells her tomatoes at the market price of $0.75 each, and no matter how many she sells, her **marginal revenue** remains $0.75.

production function

firms' output can change with each additional unit of labor or capital hired while holding one of the two variables constant

What it is: the amount a company can produce varies according to how much labor of capital is employed given a fixed amount of the other.

How it works: A firm's output initially grows at an increasing rate, then slows to a diminishing rate, and it finally decreases as it employs more labor or capital while maintaining a constant of the other resource. All these changes happen because if, for example, capital is held constant, the first workers hired can operate the capital and generate output. As more workers are hired, the workers must share more and more of the capital, leading to diminishing returns. Eventually the workers crowd out one another as they compete for the use of the firm's capital, resulting in decreasing returns.

How it is used: A teacher and his students modeled a **production function** by measuring how many paper airplanes could be produced in a minute using different numbers of students each turn.

total cost

combined expenses of a firm

What it is: the sum of all a firm's fixed and variable costs

How it works: A firm incurs a variety of costs in producing output, such as rent, wages, interest payments, utilities, transportation, and so on. The sum of all these costs is the firm's total cost. Economists calculate total cost and subtract it from all the income a firm earns to find the firm's profit. Holding all other variables constant, decreasing a firm's total cost results in increased profit for the firm.

How it is used: A company's shareholders put pressure on the CEO to cut **total cost** to increase profits.

total revenue

combined income of a firm

What it is: the product of the price of everything a firm sold multiplied by the quantity of goods sold

How it works: Total revenue is a cumulation of how much money is made from products and services sold. This revenue for a firm initially increases as the price charged increases, but it will eventually decrease as the price continues to rise. The reason total revenue increases and then decreases is because there eventually comes a price where consumers stop buying more. For example, a beach ball company sold 10,000 beach balls at a price of $10.00 per ball, earning total revenue of $100,000.

How it is used: Managers debated whether to raise or lower their prices to increase **total revenue**.

variable cost

expenses incurred only when the firm is producing output

What it is: a price that changes according to how much output a firm is producing

How it works: When firms sit idle, they incur only fixed costs, but when they produce output, they incur variable costs as well. Some of these costs are payments to and for hourly employees, raw materials, energy, transportation, maintenance of capital, marketing, distribution, and so on. Firms are always looking for ways to minimize their variable costs to remain profitable, so when production decreases, they decrease their variable costs by cutting labor and shutting down machinery to save on maintenance and energy.

How it is used: The assistant manager at the theme park started sending workers home to cut **variable costs** when a torrential rainstorm led to customers leaving.

CHAPTER 3

Degrees of Competition

Businesses compete in a variety of markets. The degree of competition in a market from these businesses has important implications for entrepreneurs, managers, and investors. Based on the level of competition, firms must decide their best size, see if they are able to set prices, figure out how to differentiate their product, consider whether to advertise, protect themselves from competitors, and sometimes even choose between competing or cooperating. Having a thorough knowledge of this competitiveness lingo will give you a solid foundation for better understanding the environment in which businesses operate.

This chapter will demystify levels of competition in an industry, how competition is measured, how competition is regulated, and the factors that ultimately determine firms' competitiveness. From *monopoly* to *perfect competition*, you will learn the terminology economists use when talking about industry and be able to apply the terms when talking with financial experts.

antitrust laws

rules to protect competition

What it is: government legislation that protects competition in different markets

How it works: As businesses grow, they have an incentive to find ways to prevent competition from other firms so they can earn bigger profits by charging higher prices. Antitrust laws are created to prohibit businesses from using unfair practices to limit competition in their industry. New firms and consumers benefit from encouraging competition because it provides for more choices of products at lower prices. For example, firms seeking to increase their profits by combining with other firms in the industry are subject to antitrust laws like the Sherman Antitrust Act and the Federal Trade Commission Act, which prohibit or regulate business combinations if they will harm other firms or consumers.

How it is used: In the 1890s and 1900s, many industries were dominated by either one or just a few firms that restricted outside competition, so the government passed **antitrust laws**.

cartel

group of producers who cooperate rather than compete

What it is: a group of businesses who have agreed to work together instead of against each other so they can earn more profit

How it works: Sometimes businesses will calculate that they can earn more profit if they cooperate with other firms, rather than compete against them. The firms will meet and work out an agreement on how to best increase their overall profit. The firms benefit by being in the cartel because their individual profit is now greater than their potential earnings if competing. Forming a cartel is illegal in the US because it results in higher prices and less competition.

How it is used: In 1960, several of the world's largest oil producers formed a **cartel** called OPEC and agreed to work together to limit the production of crude oil, maximizing their profit.

collusion

conspiracy to cheat in business

What it is: either a formal agreement or understood arrangement between firms to not compete

How it works: Collusion can be a formal agreement not to compete, or it can be tacit. For example, in the 1990s, the American company Archer Daniels Midland (ADM) formally conspired with Ajinomoto and other Japanese and Korean firms to fix the price of lysine, an ingredient in animal feed. Competition between the firms would have resulted in lysine being very inexpensive, but because they agreed not to compete, they were able to sell lysine at much higher prices in their respective regions, harming businesses and buyers. Formal collusion among firms is illegal, so ADM was prosecuted and eventually fined $70 million by the US government. Firms engage in tacit collusion when they behave cooperatively without an agreement. For example, competing gas stations may discover that when they maintain a high price for gasoline rather than lowering their price relative to their competitor, they earn more profit. So, instead of cutting their price to compete, they effectively agree to maintain high prices without ever having engaged in formal collusion.

How it is used: Two café owners were guilty of **collusion** when they secretly met to hammer out a noncompete agreement.

conglomerate

combining businesses from different industries to form a single, larger business

What it is: a form of business that competes in several unrelated industries

How it works: Firms are always trying to increase their profits and use a variety of strategies to do this. One strategy a firm may use if they find that their industry has no further room for profitable growth is to enter other industries or combine with firms in these industries to increase profits. For example, the Japanese conglomerate Yamaha Corporation competes in industries as diverse as motorcycles, boat engines, musical instruments, and sporting goods.

How it is used: A successful construction company became a **conglomerate** when it started producing cars, computers, and container ships.

copyright

legal protection over a writer, musician, or artist's original work

What it is: the exclusive right to transfer, share, or profit from your original writing, art, or music

How it works: The moment a person creates an original manuscript, or a visual or musical work, they enjoy an exclusive copyright or legal protection of that work. A copyright protects the intellectual property of the creator and allows them the ability to profit from the sale or transfer of the work. The presence of copyright protection gives people an incentive to write or create new works, which makes everyone better off. A copyright creates a legal monopoly over the work, and violation of the copyright is punishable by law. Not all countries respect each other's copyrights, resulting in plagiarism—illegal copying or sampling that denies the author the income or recognition they would otherwise receive.

How it is used: Performing someone else's play in a theater without their permission violates their **copyright** because the play belongs to them.

deadweight loss

total loss to consumers and producers when a market isn't perfectly competitive

What it is: the loss of mutually beneficial exchanges that result from imperfectly competitive markets

How it works: When a single producer with the power to set prices dominates an industry, society experiences deadweight loss, or fewer mutually beneficial exchanges than would have occurred given a competitive market. In a competitive market, the price of a good or service equals the cost of producing it plus a normal profit for the producer. When a market isn't competitive, some mutually beneficial exchanges that should have happened, now don't. Instead, the price of the product in the market is now greater than the cost of creating the product (even when including a normal profit).

The presence of deadweight loss in a market means that buyers and sellers should be better off. Economists prefer competitive markets because they minimize deadweight loss to society.

How it is used: Economists argued against a tax on imported cars because it would result in **deadweight loss**.

excess capacity

when a firm's ability to produce is greater than the demand for its product

What it is: the ability of a firm to provide more of a good or service than what's demanded because the firm is larger than necessary

How it works: When firms can charge consumers a price higher than the cost of production plus a normal profit, they can then spend some of their profit advertising and trying to differentiate themselves from near competitors. This means the firm is larger than necessary, as it can use scarce resources for something other than production. It would be more efficient if these resources being used to advertise and differentiate were instead used to produce more output.

How it is used: The sheer volume of personal injury law advertisements is an indication of **excess capacity** in that industry.

game theory

study of interdependent decision-making

What it is: the study of how a competitor makes decisions given the other competitor's possible decisions

How it works: In the context of economics, game theory is used to understand how firms make decisions when their profits are dependent upon the firm's competitors. For example, assume there are two competing lemonade stands in a neighborhood. One owner, Malik, observes that his profits decrease when he lowers his price below the other owner's, Sasha's, but increase when he keeps his prices the same as hers. Sasha observes that her profits increase when she matches Malik's price but decrease when she raises her price relative to his. Using game theory, Malik and Sasha independently conclude that they should charge the same price for lemonade.

How it is used: Instead of supply and demand analysis, economists use **game theory** to understand firms' decisions in markets dominated by just a few businesses.

geographic monopoly

the only seller of an item in an area

What it is: when there is only one provider of a good or service in an area

How it works: Some places are remote and don't provide much opportunity for profit, so if a firm already exists in that area, competitors have little incentive to enter the area to compete. When this provider has the only business, they have a geographic monopoly. For example, in the Desert Southwest region of the US, it is not uncommon to observe a single gas station hundreds of miles from the next nearest station. In this case, the gas station has a geographic monopoly because it has no close competition. Geographic monopoly allows the firm to charge a higher price for their good or service than if there were nearby competitors.

How it is used: Ned decided to open a convenience store on a deserted stretch of highway in Nevada, thinking he could make a hefty profit as a **geographic monopoly**.

government monopoly

only the government can sell it

What it is: the government is the only producer of a good or service

How it works: Governments may from time to time think it is in the best interest of their citizens to be the only producer of a good or service, creating a government monopoly. For example, in Mexico prior to 2023, all fuel was sold by the state-owned monopoly PEMEX. No other companies in the country or from outside was allowed to sell fuel to consumers. Government monopolies are unpopular with consumers because there are no alternatives provided by private firms.

How it is used: In many countries, the national airline is a **government monopoly** supported by both ticket sales and taxes.

Herfindahl-Hirschman Index (HHI)

measure of relative firm size and competition in an industry

What it is: a formula calculating the size of firms relative to the size of their industry, or market share, as a measure of the level of competition in that industry

How it works: Government regulators use the HHI to measure the possible effects of combining two or more firms in competition in an industry. High index numbers tell us that there will be too much concentration of power by one or more firms in the industry, so the firms in it will have too much control over prices for the industry to be considered competitive. Low index numbers tell us that the industry is competitive, which is better for consumers. When two or more firms are considering a merge in an already concentrated industry, regulators can block the merge if the predicted HHI is too large.

How it is used: A merger between two large firms was blocked by the Federal Trade Commission when government economists calculated that the **Herfindahl-Hirschman Index** would increase by 3,000.

horizontal merger

combining two or more competitors to make a new, larger firm

What it is: a combination formed when competing companies join together

How it works: A combination of two or more firms in the same industry and at the same level of production is considered a horizontal merger. One way for firms to increase their profitability is to combine with other similar firms so they can have more power over prices. By combining their operations, the firms can increase their total output and eliminate their redundancies to become more efficient. For example, United Airlines and Continental Airlines formed a horizontal merger when the two airlines combined.

How it is used: Malik and Sasha each owned lemonade stands in a busy neighborhood and decided they would be more profitable if they combined to form a **horizontal merger**.

imperfect competition
condition where firms have pricing power

What it is: markets in which firms can set prices

How it works: There are different levels of competition in industries, and when firms in an industry have some power over their products' prices, imperfect competition exists. Most industries in the US experience some level of imperfect competition, where firms in the industry can either differentiate their products from those of their competitors, or they are able to make products at a lower cost. This ability to differentiate or operate at lower cost allows them some control over the price they charge for their products, making them more profitable. This ability to set prices is sometimes offset by the fact that there are close substitutes for their product.

How it is used: The automobile industry has **imperfect competition** because automakers can make their cars look different from their competitors and thus charge a higher price for them.

interdependence
businesses relying on other businesses' actions

What it is: when a firm's behavior is dependent on its competition's behavior and vice versa

How it works: Interdependence means that firms consider the actions of other firms when making production decisions. In industries where a few firms control a large portion of the overall market, they typically do not act independently. Instead, they consider how their competitors will respond to their decisions and how they will respond to their competitors' decisions. Firms behaving interdependently look at all the possible courses of action they can take and then weigh that against their assumptions of other firms' actions.

How it is used: When the company's board of directors met, they carefully considered all the ways their competitor would respond to a new business strategy being proposed because the industry was marked by **interdependence**.

monopolistic competition

industry where firms compete by making their products appear slightly different from the competition

What it is: a market where competitors try to differentiate themselves and their products, rather than competing on price

How it works: Monopolistic competition happens when firms in an industry try to make themselves (and their products) appear different than their competition. For example, in the fast-food industry, competitors all offer a quick meal at a relatively low price, but they use a combination of different ingredients, delivery methods, styles of cooking, and advertising to make themselves appear different than the competition. This ability to differentiate gives them some power over the price of their products, limited by the fact that close alternatives exist.

How it is used: An advertising firm looking to increase profits by offering its services to new industries determined that ones with **monopolistic competition** offered more probable clients than industries offering generic goods.

monopoly

one-firm industry

What it is: an industry where one firm produces all the output

How it works: A monopoly exists when a single firm produces all the output in an industry, completely dominating it. Monopoly is the opposite of perfect competition. Because the company that has a monopoly over something faces no competition from other firms, their ability to set prices and make economic profits is limited only by consumer demand and the government. As such, most forms of monopoly are illegal in the US because they cause more harm than good. In rare cases, monopolies are permitted but face government regulation over prices.

How it is used: In the late 1800s and early 1900s, the oil industry in the US was the Standard Oil Company, a **monopoly** owned by John D. Rockefeller.

Nash equilibrium

condition where a firm has no reason to change their strategy

What it is: in economics, a condition that exists in a two-firm industry when neither competitor can benefit by changing their business strategy

How it works: Most of the time, firms are profit maximizers and will pursue strategies that yield the highest profit independent of what other firms are doing. However, given an industry dominated by two competing firms, the total profits in the industry may be less than what is possible because of interdependent decision-making. In this case, the firms consider their competition's strategy and choose their best response given the other's decision, and this may or may not coincide with maximum possible profit. This phenomenon is the Nash equilibrium.

How it is used: Two competing firms found themselves in a **Nash equilibrium** when neither had an incentive to change their pricing strategy, given the other firm's pricing strategy.

natural monopoly

when a single firm can produce cheaper output than a combination of smaller firms

What it is: sometimes a single producer is allowed to produce all an industry's output because they can do it cheaper than if there was competition

How it works: A natural monopoly exists when a firm is so large and efficient that it can produce output at a lower cost than would a combination of smaller firms producing the same amount of output, effectively eliminating competition. In some cities and towns, for example, the electric utility company is a natural monopoly because it can generate electricity at lower cost with a single power plant than could a bunch of competing companies with smaller power plants. Governments allow natural monopolies because of their efficiency, but the government regulates these businesses' prices to protect consumers. A natural monopoly's sheer scale and size make it hard for any new firms to effectively compete against them.

How it is used: Railroads connecting different cities are often **natural monopolies** because it would not make economic sense to build another railroad connecting the same places.

non-price competition
firms competing on something other than price

What it is: when firms compete based on real or perceived differences between their products and their rivals', rather than offering a cheaper substitute

How it works: Non-price competition involves a firm convincing their buyers that what they're selling is unique from all others in the market. A firm's success at non-price competition depends on how well the firm can convince consumers that their product is worth the extra price. Although non-price competition results in higher prices, consumers tend to like the greater variety of goods offered in markets where non-price competition exists.

How it is used: Apple growers may offer different varieties of apples, or emphasize their origin, which are both forms of **non-price competition.**

oligopoly
industry dominated by a few firms

What it is: an industry where a few firms control a significant portion of the market

How it works: As industries age, firms within an industry grow, combine, or cease to exist. Given enough time, only a few large businesses will be left. They will use their size and market power to prevent new firms from entering, and they will also compete with existing firms interdependently. This is called an oligopoly. For example, the domestic airline industry in the US is an oligopoly. American, Delta, Southwest, and United account for about 70% of the market share in the domestic airline market. These firms consider what the other firms are doing when making business decisions and compete both on price and non-price factors. Their collective size and scale make it difficult for new airlines to enter the market and compete nationally.

How it is used: An economics student determined streaming video platforms such as Netflix, Disney+, Amazon Prime Video, and Hulu are an **oligopoly** because the firms dominate the market.

patent

legal protection over inventions

What it is: when people invent new technologies, they can seek to protect the invention from being copied by applying for this legal paperwork from the government

How it works: A patent allows the patent holder the exclusive right to profit from the sale of their invention. Inventors can apply for a patent and then sell the rights to use the patent to other people or businesses, making those people or businesses now the patent holders. Patent protection provides an incentive for people and businesses to do research and development because it gives the patent holder a monopoly over the technology for a limited time. During the time that the patent protection exists, the patent holder may earn monopoly profits to recoup their investment in research and development.

How it is used: Pharmaceutical companies invest billions of dollars in research and development every year on new medical treatments, **patent** them, and then earn monopoly profits from their sale.

perfect competition

market where firms have no control over price

What it is: a highly competitive market in which all firms sell basically the same thing and in which no single firm has pricing power

How it works: In perfectly competitive markets, price is determined by supply and demand. Firms only can choose how much they can produce and sell at the market price. In addition, buyers and sellers know everything about the goods or services being sold. Economists refer to firms in perfectly competitive markets as price takers, and this feature is what makes perfectly competitive markets different from other forms of market where firms have some power over prices. Finally, businesses that participate in perfectly competitive markets only earn normal profits, which does not invite further competition.

How it is used: An economics student realized that **perfect competition** may exist in the local farmers' market because the carrots were all identical and sold at the same price no matter which farmer's stand she visited.

perfect information
condition where buyers and sellers know everything

What it is: when, in highly competitive markets, every producer and consumer knows all information about the product, the costs involved in producing it, and at what price it should sell

How it works: When buyers and sellers have perfect information, neither has power to offer or charge a price different from the price determined by the market. For example, lemonade from a child's neighborhood lemonade stand is easy to understand in terms of what the product is, as well as how much it should cost to produce. When perfect information does not exist, then businesses are often able to charge higher prices, as customers do not know how much it cost to produce the good. Automobile manufacturers know much more about their vehicles and the costs associated with producing them than the average consumer, giving the manufacturer an information advantage as well as pricing power.

How it is used: Some economists believe that **perfect information** exists in the stock market because so many different investors buying and selling shares of a company's stock have an idea of the company's expected future earnings.

price discrimination
charging different consumers different prices for the same thing

What it is: when a market is not competitive, a producer may be able to charge customers different prices for the same good or service

How it works: If there are no close substitutes for a good or service, a seller may choose to charge different customers varying prices based on their willingness to pay. Generally, price discrimination is against the law, but some forms are allowed. For example, restaurants, movie theaters, and theme parks practice price discrimination when they sell meals or tickets at lower prices for children, senior citizens, or military veterans, while charging everyone else a higher price for the same thing.

How it is used: A dance club practiced **price discrimination** when it only charged an entry fee to men and called it ladies' night.

price leadership

ability of a firm to initiate price changes for an entire industry

What it is: when there is not much competition in a market, a firm may have the power to raise or lower prices before their competition

How it works: Price leadership allows a firm to increase their profits at the expense of the competition or price followers. By being the first to raise or lower prices, the firm can strategically drive out other firms and capture a bigger share of the market. For example, assume American Airlines has price leadership in the airline industry. American can then use this advantage to raise or lower ticket prices when it is most profitable for them or most costly for their competition.

How it is used: A successful fund manager determined that some businesses she was looking to invest in had **price leadership** and chose to only invest in those.

prisoner's dilemma

condition where two firms would be better off cooperating rather than competing

What it is: when two competing firms would choose a different strategy if they knew in advance how the other firm would respond to their strategy

How it works: In a prisoner's dilemma, both firms end up choosing a strategy that does not maximize profits because they are unaware of the other firm's behavior. The term comes from a classic example in crime dramas where two suspects are interrogated separately and unable to communicate with each other. Each would be better off if they remained silent—they would go free if neither confesses—but the police tell them that, if they confess while their fellow suspect remains silent, the confessor will receive a light prison sentence while the silent partner will receive a longer prison sentence. Not knowing what their partner chooses, both have an incentive to confess to avoid the longer prison sentence, and the police get the confessions.

How it is used: Two competing firms found themselves in a **prisoner's dilemma** when they chose to charge a low price for their product, since they could've both charged a higher price and earned more.

technological monopoly

patent or copyright protects a firm from competition

What it is: when a business can take advantage of their protected intellectual property to be the only firm in a market

How it works: Patent or copyright protection gives a business the legal right to be the sole producer of a good or service. This is a technological monopoly. When firms have a technological monopoly, they can earn much more profit than if they faced competition, so this gives firms the incentive to do research and development. For example, Apple has a technological monopoly over its devices and operating systems, so developers must pay Apple when they create a program or application to be sold in the Apple Store.

How it is used: A brilliant inventor became very wealthy when his patent gave him a **technological monopoly**.

vertical integration

combining businesses from different stages of production into one

What it is: a firm created by fusing smaller firms from different steps in the production process

How it works: A business may determine that it can be more profitable if it combines with other businesses in the same industry, but at different stages of the production process, because it will have more control over costs by avoiding "the middleman." This combining process is called vertical integration. An example is when Andrew Carnegie vertically integrated his steel manufacturing company by buying an iron ore mining company and shipping company. This way, he had access to raw materials and ways to deliver product.

How it is used: A child applied **vertical integration** when she saved her allowance, bought a dozen potted lemon trees, and used their lemons to make lemonade to sell directly to customers.

CHAPTER 4

Market Failures

Markets generally do a good job of allocating goods and services to the people who want them, but sometimes they fail to produce certain things, or they create unintended side effects that affect neither buyer nor seller. When this happens, economists refer to it as a market failure. Economists then try to solve the market failure in a way that is most efficient for society. They analyze not only the internal costs and benefits of markets for producers and consumers but also look at the external costs and benefits to society. Whether it is providing public goods, managing externalities, or applying the Coase theorem, market failures and their possible solutions introduce us to vocabulary that further increases our understanding of economics.

Coase theorem

negative side effects of production affecting private property owners are best negotiated between the producer and the property owner

What it is: a baseline for understanding how to best deal with negative economic side effects to production

How it works: The Coase theorem illustrates how those harmed by a negative side effect of a business can negotiate a payment to offset the side effect. The theorem assumes that producers and the people negatively affected by those producers can negotiate a payment to offset the negative side effect. The Coase theorem relies on there being little cost associated with negotiating and that the producer and those affected have access to all the information available about the problem. If these conditions are not met, then the Coase theorem only gives us a starting point for finding a solution to the problem.

How it is used: A homeowner with a beautiful view of the ocean applied the **Coase theorem** when they bought the property across the street from the developer who had planned to build a beach rental condominium, blocking the homeowner's view.

externality

costs or benefits from a market exchange born by neither producer nor consumer

What it is: an unintended consequence of a transaction between a buyer and seller that affects people external to the transaction

How it works: Sometimes people who are neither the buyer nor seller are affected by a product. Externalities can be good, bad, or both. Markets that produce externalities may be either producing too much of a good or service, or else not enough. Economists recommend intervening in markets that produce externalities so that the amount produced provides the most benefit to society.

How it is used: When a city hosts the Olympics, they need to consider not only the costs and benefits to sports venues and local businesses involved with the games but also **externalities** like increased traffic congestion and pollution.

free-rider problem

businesses are reluctant to provide a good or service if they cannot restrict people who do not pay from consuming it

What it is: the idea that businesses will not typically provide a good or service if they cannot withhold it from those who do not pay

How it works: Businesses like to make money from what they're providing—and will not typically do things for free. For example, a private business has little incentive to pay for an open access road because it is too easy for non-payers to use it. Private businesses will, however, build a limited access toll road because they can restrict its use to only those who pay. Nothing is actually free, because somebody always has to pay when using scarce resources and often it ends up being taxpayers. Governments must then provide the goods and services that face the free-rider problem.

How it is used: Sometimes taxpayers and businesses must pay the cost for someone else's healthcare because emergency rooms face the **free-rider problem** and cannot restrict access to treatment to just paying customers.

marginal private benefit

benefit specifically to a consumer from an additional unit of consumption

What it is: the amount of additional value received only by a consumer directly involved in a market transaction

How it works: When we buy a good or service, typically we are the ones reaping the benefit. For example, if someone buys a candy bar, then they get the benefit of consuming it. If this benefit is not shared with anyone else, it is completely internal to the consumer and is thus private. If, however, others benefit from the buyer's consumption, then there is an external benefit not accounted for in the transaction.

How it is used: If the **marginal private benefit** of getting vaccinated for the flu is less than the benefit to society, then not enough vaccinations are being consumed.

marginal private cost

cost paid by a firm to produce an additional unit of output

What it is: the costs born only by the producer in making an additional unit of output

How it works: When a firm produces an additional unit, they face private costs in producing it (like labor, machinery, and raw materials). For example, when an electric utility burns coal to make electricity, they must pay for the labor, machinery, and coal to produce the additional unit of electricity. If the costs of producing electricity are not shared with anyone else, the costs are considered private and internal. If, however, other people bear some of the cost of producing electricity, like not being able to breathe clean air, then there is an additional cost not being accounted for in the transaction.

How it is used: A noisy bar in an otherwise quiet neighborhood experienced **marginal private costs** less than the total cost to society because noise pollution was not factored into their costs.

marginal social benefit

benefit to society of consuming an additional unit of output

What it is: whenever a person consumes a good or service, it not only provides the person with a private benefit but also provides society an additional benefit because the person is a member of society

How it works: Marginal social benefit is the concept that the benefit you get from an item or service provides a (hopefully positive) benefit for society. Sometimes the marginal social benefit is not the same as the benefit to the individual. For example, when a person consumes cigarettes in a public setting, the additional benefit to them may be greater than the marginal social benefit because many people hate cigarette smoke. On the other hand, when a person consumes a flu vaccine, not only does the individual benefit but also there is a greater marginal social benefit to the unvaccinated in being around the consumer because they are now less likely to get sick.

How it is used: Governments often use tax credits or direct payments to people to encourage consumption of goods and services with a **marginal social benefit** greater than its marginal private benefit.

marginal social cost
cost to society of producing an additional unit of output

What it is: whenever a firm produces a good or service, it not only incurs a private cost for the business but also incurs an additional cost to society because the firm is a part of society

How it works: The concept of marginal social cost is that when businesses produce something, there is a cost to society and not just the business. Sometimes the marginal social cost is not the same as the private cost to the firm. For example, when a business produces pollution as a side effect of production, the marginal social cost may be greater than the private cost to the firm because the firm may not necessarily pay for the harm caused to people and the environment. In cases like this, governments will regulate production to reduce the marginal social cost so that it equals the marginal social benefit.

How it is used: The **marginal social cost** of pollution was much greater than the private cost to the company that off-loaded their pollutants to the public's clean water supply.

non-excludable
something that cannot be withheld from people who do not pay

What it is: goods and services that can be acquired without having to pay for them

How it works: When a good or service is non-excludable—that is, it's free or doesn't require payment—there is not much incentive to produce it because firms cannot profit from it. For example, ensuring that there is adequate police and fire protection in a community will likely not be provided by private firms because there's no way to make this profitable. Instead, non-excludable goods and services are often provided by the government at taxpayers' expense.

How it is used: Sunlight is a **non-excludable** energy source because all have access to it without having to pay.

non-rival

something where one person's consumption does not limit another person's consumption of the same thing

What it is: a good or service that can be consumed by many people at the same time

How it works: Non-rival goods or services may be taken advantage of by multiple people at once. For example, listening to a concert or watching a movie are non-rival because one person's consumption doesn't limit others' experiences. There is a limit to non-rivalry for some goods and services. In the example, this limit could be seats in a movie theater or concert venue. Markets will only provide non-rival goods if they can make them excludable to those who do not pay.

How it is used: Watching fireworks on July 4th is **non-rival** because one person's enjoyment does not limit other people's enjoyment.

pollution permit

a way to limit harm to the planet by selling a fixed number of licenses

What it is: a license to emit a certain amount of harm to nature in exchange for payment

How it works: Instead of taxing all polluters equally, government-issued pollution permits (which give the owners permission to pollute) incentivize firms to be efficient and create less waste by creating a market for the permits. For example, a firm that has found a cleaner way to produce can sell their permits to the competition and make additional profit, while also reducing their emissions. If people are concerned about the environment, they can purchase permits and not use them, thus preventing some pollution. By reducing the number of permits available, scarcity grows, costs for polluting firms increase, and they are further incentivized not to pollute.

How it is used: A class of elementary students in New Jersey raised money and bought a **pollution permit** to prevent tons of sulfur dioxide and carbon dioxide from entering the atmosphere.

pollution tax

tax on firms that pollute

What it is: the government may place a tax on firms in a pollution-producing industry to curb pollution and raise government revenue

How it works: The pollution tax is placed on all firms in an industry to reduce production and, as a result, pollution. The problem with pollution taxes is they are levied on all firms in an industry equally, thus punishing heavy polluting businesses as well as efficient and green businesses. Many argue that it's better to sell licenses, which would allow all firms in an industry to emit a certain amount of pollution. Heavy polluters would then face higher costs than light polluters.

How it is used: A local government was considering options for reducing air pollution in their city and decided to place a **pollution tax** on all firms that emit sulfur dioxide and other volatile organic compounds.

positive externality

an unintended benefit to society from a market transaction

What it is: an exchange between buyer and seller in a market creates an unintended benefit to society

How it works: Sometimes private consumption of a good or service provides benefits to others not involved in the transaction. For example, when a homeowner pays a landscape architect to make the front yard look better, not only do the homeowner and architect benefit, but the neighbors also benefit from having a prettier neighborhood (which might even increase the value of their own homes). When positive externalities exist, government may pay consumers or producers a subsidy to increase the market's output.

How it is used: A local beekeeper was hired by a farmer to help pollinate his orchard, but the bees created a **positive externality** when they also pollinated adjacent orchards as well.

public good

item or service that markets have little incentive to provide

What it is: governments provide certain items and services that markets are unable or unwilling to provide

How it works: When a good or service is non-excludable and non-rival, usually governments must provide it. These goods or services, called public goods, are often only produced by the government because they cannot be withheld from non-payers, and/or they can be used by many people at once. For example, cities provide police protection to the community in exchange for taxes because private firms don't have an incentive to do so. Sometimes the distinction between private goods and public goods is harder to define, meaning you might see both in the market. For example, public education is offered to all families regardless of their ability to pay, while private education is offered only to those families willing and able to pay for it.

How it is used: The interstate highway system is a **public good** because anyone can drive on it even if they don't pay.

regulation

rules for people and businesses made by the government

What it is: government creates laws that impact individuals and companies, ultimately affecting markets

How it works: One way for governments to address market failures is to create rules affecting buyers and sellers. For example, in the early 1900s, meat-packing firms allowed for all kinds of food contamination and unsafe practices because it costs money to maintain safe and sanitary factories. In response to the novel *The Jungle* by Upton Sinclair, people became more aware of the conditions, and this prompted the government to regulate the food industry to ensure cleaner, safer food.

How it is used: Many business owners dislike **regulation** because the government's rules make running their businesses more expensive.

socially optimal

market condition that maximizes benefit to society

What it is: markets do not always provide maximum benefit to society because of unintended consequences, so government may try to influence the behavior of buyers or sellers in such a way that the benefit to society is greater

How it works: When there are unintended side effects created by markets, governments will intervene in the market to adjust the amount being produced to what is best for society. For example, if vaccines create a benefit to society greater than the benefit to just the patient and the pharmaceutical company, then government may pay either consumers or producers to increase the number of vaccines administered.

How it is used: The amount of pollution being created in the 1970s was not **socially optimal** because bystanders were harmed by large corporations' actions, so government stepped in to reduce pollution's effects.

subsidy

government payment to a seller or buyer

What it is: when a government wants more of a good or service, they will sometimes pay an amount to producers or consumers as encouragement

How it works: One way governments can encourage firms to produce more is to provide either producers or consumers with a subsidy. By subsidizing an industry, more is produced at a lower price to consumers. This is either because the business can provide the good for less, or because the consumer gets money to pay for part of the good. The purpose of the subsidy might be to ensure an optimal quantity in the market in case of a market failure. For example, research and development of new medicines may be subsidized by the government to increase the total amount of new medications in the market.

How it is used: Farmers received a **subsidy** for growing corn, so production increased substantially.

CHAPTER 5

Resource Markets

Like goods and services, resources are exchanged in markets. Raw materials, labor, and machinery are exchanged in something called a resource market. Resource markets are like other types of markets in many ways, but when it comes to the resource market for labor, there are some key differences. Unlike goods, labor is made up of people, who respond to incentives. A banana does not care how much you pay for it, but a human being does. This and the relationship between labor and employers involves a lot of economic jargon. This chapter will define terms describing the way workers and employers interact in the labor market and different classifications of labor and factors affecting the supply and demand for labor.

arbitration

system where an independent judge settles disputes between employers and workers

What it is: when workers are hired, they may sign a contract with an employer that says that any future disputes will be settled by an independent judge rather than in a court of law

How it works: To minimize court costs, firms will often have employees agree to binding arbitration in their employment contract. By doing this, they agree that they must settle disagreements with a third party, as sometimes these disagreements cannot be otherwise settled between employer and employee. In arbitration, the different parties present their argument and any evidence to an independent judge who then makes a decision that both parties have already pre-agreed to accept. Arbitration has the benefit of being cheaper and quicker than a lawsuit in court.

How it is used: A disgruntled employee threatened to sue the company over a disagreement about their paycheck but was rejected by a lawyer because the employee had already agreed to **arbitration** instead.

collective bargaining

workers negotiating with their employer as a group rather than individually

What it is: instead of negotiating employment contracts on an individual basis, a group of workers appoint a representative to negotiate on their entire behalf

How it works: Usually there is an imbalance in power between an individual employee and an entire company in a wage negotiation because the company has more information and resources, thus holding an advantage. Collective bargaining is a way to make things more equal between workers and employers by combining the demands of all workers in the negotiation with the threat of a strike or slowdown if workers' demands are not met.

How it is used: Dissatisfied workers discovered that when they combined their efforts by using **collective bargaining**, they were able to increase their wages.

competitive labor market

market for workers where wages and employment are determined by supply and demand

What it is: when there are many employers and potential employees, supply and demand for labor determines the market wage, and firms can hire as many workers as necessary at that wage

How it works: Competitive labor markets exist when there is a sufficiently large enough labor force and number of employers in an industry. Supply and demand determine the market wage and level of employment in a competitive labor market. As demand for labor increases, wages and employment increase. However, as demand for labor decreases, wages fall and fewer people are employed. Additionally, when the supply of labor increases, wages fall and employment increases. However, as supply of labor decreases, wages increase and employment decreases.

How it is used: It is difficult for Angela to increase her wages in a **competitive labor market** because there are so many others willing to work at the market wage.

cost-minimizing input combination

cheapest mix of labor and capital necessary to produce a certain amount

What it is: blending labor and capital to produce a certain amount of output at the lowest possible cost

How it works: Firms have choices regarding how much capital and labor to employ when producing a certain amount of output. The combination producing the same amount of output at lowest cost helps businesses maximize profits; this is called the cost-minimizing input combination.

Firms have different ways to calculate this combination. They may consider how much output they want to produce and then compare different combinations of labor and capital producing that amount, choosing the combination with the lowest cost. Another way firms can determine the cost-minimizing input combination is equating the ratios of the productivity of the last worker hired to the wage rate and the productivity of the last unit of capital employed to the cost of capital.

How it is used: Retail stores try to use a **cost-minimizing input combination** when determining how many cashiers to employ and how many self-checkout registers to purchase.

derived demand
need for products creates need for land, labor, and capital

What it is: a deep need for goods and services produced in an economy creates a requirement for the resources to make those goods and services

How it works: Product markets and resource markets are necessarily connected because you cannot have one without the other; this phenomenon is derived demand. When demand for goods and services changes, the demand for the land, labor, and capital needed to make those goods must change as well. For example, increased demand for potatoes increases the need for the land, farmers, and equipment needed to grow potatoes. This derived demand directly affects rents, wages, and interest payments on the resources used.

How it is used: Demand for books creates **derived demand** for authors, editors, designers, computers, and printers.

efficiency wage
paying people above-market wages to incentivize hard work

What it is: an employer will sometimes pay their workers a higher wage than what similar employers are paying to encourage higher productivity

How it works: Employers know that workers are not always as productive as they could be, and employees know that they can work elsewhere at a similar wage if they choose. Efficiency wages encourage worker productivity because employees now realize they are getting paid more than earnings at other employers, giving them the incentive to work harder to keep their job. The presence of efficiency wages may lead to higher rates of unemployment because unexpected people enter the labor force and hope to earn these above-market wages.

How it is used: A local restaurant chain paid **efficiency wages** to attract loyal, productive workers and to minimize turnover.

factor market

market for raw materials, labor, and capital

What it is: the market where firms hire labor and purchase raw materials and capital

How it works: In economies with private property, households own the factors of production and sell them to firms in the factor market (also called the resource market). In exchange for the resources, firms pay the households rent, wages, interest, and profit. For example, when a high school student begins applying for jobs, they are effectively offering to sell their labor in the factor market to the businesses to which they applied.

How it is used: In the **factor market**, a professor sold his labor to a nearby university in exchange for a salary, and he collected rental income from the firm pumping off crude oil from his ranch.

lockout

strategy of voluntarily shutting down a business

What it is: a strategy used by employers when negotiating with workers to accept their wage offer or not work at all

How it works: If an employer does not agree to union wage demands, they may decide to shut down their business temporarily or even hire nonunion workers and lock out the union until workers accept the employer's offer. The premise of a lockout is that the business can outlast the workers because it can survive the temporary loss of income. For example, in 1998–1999, the National Basketball Association (NBA) owners locked out the players when the players' union demanded higher wages and management refused to pay.

How it is used: When a group of workers in a union demanded higher wages, the company decided on a **lockout** of union workers until they reduced their demands.

low-wage labor

work that does not require any specialized skills to perform

What it is: jobs that can be learned in a day and only require effort

How it works: Certain entry-level jobs do not require the worker to have any specialized skills or training and can typically be learned in a day; these jobs are considered low-wage labor (also called unskilled labor). For example, bagging groceries, busing tables, mowing yards, and basic factory work are low-wage labor because there are many people able to do the work relative to the number of these types of jobs available.

How it is used: Many people learn the basics of showing up on time and earning a paycheck when they perform **low-wage labor** in their youth.

marginal factor cost

price of employing an additional worker or machine

What it is: the price a firm pays for an additional worker or piece of equipment

How it works: Marginal factor cost is the cost of one extra employee or machine. The price per unit paid for labor or capital is determined by who/what is available in the market. If the market is competitive, firms can hire as much labor and capital as needed without driving up their price. If, however, the market is not competitive, then each additional unit of labor and capital hired is more expensive than the previous unit. For example, assume that there is a town with one factory. If the factory wants to hire more workers, it will have to offer a higher wage to attract additional labor; it will also have to pay the existing workers that higher wage, driving up the firm's marginal factor cost.

How it is used: A bright economics student realized that her hourly wage as a lifeguard was a **marginal factor cost** for the neighborhood pool.

marginal product of capital

change in output caused by adding a piece of equipment

What it is: a measure of how adding machinery and equipment changes a firm's total output of goods or services

How it works: Each additional unit of capital a firm purchases contributes to their total output; this concept is the marginal product of capital. However, for each additional machine, you get less value. For example, an eager-to-grow computer company discovers that the marginal product of capital is 5 additional computers when it adds a second robot to their assembly line, but when a third robot is added, it only supplies 2 additional computers. Firms use the marginal product of capital to help them to calculate the combination of labor and machinery that maximizes profits.

How it is used: A firm decided to remove machinery from their factory when they calculated that the **marginal product of capital** was negative.

marginal product of labor

change in output caused by adding a worker

What it is: a measure of how adding workers changes a firm's total output of goods or services

How it works: Each additional unit of labor hired contributes to the firm's total output; this concept is the marginal product of labor. However, for each additional laborer, you get less value. For example, an enterprising restaurant discovers that the marginal product of labor is 5 additional meals served per day when it adds a second cook to the kitchen, but this diminishes to 2 more meals when a third cook is added, as they share equipment. Firms consider the marginal product of labor to help them find the combination of labor and machinery that maximizes profits.

How it is used: A firm realized that it should have stopped hiring additional labor when the **marginal product of labor** from hiring the last worker was zero.

marginal revenue product

change in a firm's total income caused by adding an additional worker or machine

What it is: the price of the last unit sold multiplied by the amount of output generated by adding an additional labor or capital resource to a firm

How it works: A business makes the most profit when they hire additional workers until their contribution to revenue equals the cost of hiring the last worker. For example, when a firm's marginal revenue product is greater than the cost of adding an additional worker, it makes sense to add a worker, but the firm should stop adding labor once the marginal revenue product equals the wage of the last worker hired.

How it is used: A baseball manufacturer calculated its **marginal revenue product** as $50 when they determined that the last worker produced 10 additional baseballs, which sold at $5 per baseball.

mediation

when an independent intermediary helps employers and workers reach an agreement by having both sides listen to each other's concerns and come up with a joint solution

What it is: a way to resolve conflicts by reaching a compromise with the help of an impartial judge called a mediator

How it works: In professional situations, mediation, or supervised listening and problem-solving, is sometimes a requirement of a contract. To minimize court costs, businesses add this to employment contracts to settle disagreements that cannot be otherwise settled between employer and employee. In mediation, the different parties present their arguments and any evidence to each other and to a mediator who then helps both parties decide. Mediation has the benefit of being cheaper and quicker than a lawsuit in court.

How it is used: When Laura went to **mediation**, she learned a lot from her employer's perspective, and they worked together to create a solution benefiting them both.

monopsony

market with a single consumer

What it is: a market where all the sellers produce for a single buyer

How it works: Sometimes either government or a large firm dominates a product market or resource market as the single consumer of goods, services, or resources. In this case, it would be a monopsony. For example, in some small towns, a single factory employs all the labor in the town. A monopsonist in the labor market employs less labor and at a lower wage because, unlike competitive labor markets, the single firm's price of hiring an additional worker is determined by the last worker hired, so the profit-maximizing quantity of labor is less than in competition.

How it is used: Many young people leave their small hometowns in search of better wages elsewhere when the only jobs in town are working for a **monopsony**.

skilled labor

workers with specialized training

What it is: workers who have specific skills and training to perform their work

How it works: Skilled labor requires training and a combination of physical labor and mental problem-solving. For example, electricians, plumbers, welders, and certified mechanics do work that requires significant training, and they earn higher wages for their work than do low-wage laborers. Skilled labors' ability to earn relatively higher wages is the result of their relative scarcity compared to market demand for their skills and ability. People seeking to become skilled labor need certifications and training provided by either technical schools or through apprenticeships with accomplished skilled workers.

How it is used: People who like physical labor but also like problem-solving and mentally stimulating work should consider becoming **skilled labor**.

strike

when a group of workers refuse to work until their demands are met

What it is: one strategy of labor unions to get higher wages is to threaten to stop working en masse and carry it out if their demands are not met

How it works: A strike is when employees band together and stop working for a cause. When labor goes on strike, the affected business will struggle to produce output and take financial losses. The mere threat of a strike is often enough to make an employer more willing to meet the demands of labor. For example, airlines take significant losses if they do not operate daily. So, when pilots, flight attendants, or ground crews go on strike, the airline must cease operations, motivating the airline to reach an agreement with the striking workers.

How it is used: Parents of students must find childcare or stay home from work when teachers go on **strike**, because the schools are closed.

union
organized labor

What it is: an association of workers who negotiate employment, wages, and benefits collectively rather than individually

How it works: In general, there is an imbalance of power between an individual worker and an entire company when it comes to negotiating their employment contract, wages, and benefits. This is why workers may form a union and negotiate with the employer as a group to secure higher wages and better benefits. The union is funded by member dues and uses those funds to pay for professional negotiators and to support union members when they are on strike. For example, the United Auto Workers, or UAW, is a union that negotiates on behalf of autoworkers across much of the US.

How it is used: Cesar Chavez and others formed the UFW (United Farm Workers) **union** to negotiate better pay and benefits on behalf of farmworkers.

wage
payment for labor

What it is: when people supply their labor in exchange for a payment

How it works: Wages are money paid for work and can be hourly, project based, or in the form of a salary. Hourly wages are calculated by taking the number of hours worked during a specific period multiplied by the hourly wage rate. Workers can also be paid a wage based on completing a certain project regardless of how long it might take. In addition, wages can be paid in the form of a salary, where the worker earns a fixed payment at a regular interval regardless of the number of hours worked. Wages are the primary source of income for most households in the US, and they are the primary cost of business for most firms.

How it is used: When Katie finally graduated from college and got a job as an engineer, she was surprised how much her **wage** had increased from her days as a waitress.

wage taker

competitive firms that can employ as many workers as they need at the market wage without causing it to change

What it is: in competitive labor markets, firms can hire as much labor as they need at the market wage

How it works: When there are many workers available and many firms competing to hire them, any individual firm has little control over the market wage. Therefore, competitive firms in competitive labor markets employ as much labor as they need without causing the market wage to change and therefore are wage takers. For example, in a large city, fast-food restaurants can hire as many workers as they need at the market wage rate in the city for that kind of work. If they offer less, they will struggle to fill jobs, and if they offer more, they will face unnecessary higher labor costs than their competition, so they take the market wage and offer that to applicants.

How it is used: An engineering firm was not attracting many applicants when they offered below-market wages to reduce costs, so their economist advised them they were a **wage taker** and should instead offer the market wage to attract job seekers.

CHAPTER 6

Economic Measurement

The economy in which we live is complex. So one way economists try to better understand the economy (and all of the relationships in it) is by measuring a variety of factors like economic output, prices, and employment. These economists then create economic models to explain the relationships between the measures so they can understand how they all relate, provide policymakers with solutions to economic problems, and identify possible side effects to the solutions. From the *business cycle* to the *natural rate of unemployment* to the *Phillips curve*, an entire vocabulary is dedicated to the measurement and understanding of the key variables in the economy.

aggregate demand

households', firms', governments', and the rest of the world's willingness and ability to purchase an economy's output at various price levels

What it is: the combined demand for an economy's output from all sectors in the economy

How it works: Aggregate demand (sometimes notated as AD) is the total demand for an economy's output throughout the economy. More output is demanded at a lower price level and less output is demanded at a higher price level. Changes in spending by households, businesses, government, and the rest of the world result in direct changes in aggregate demand. Holding all other factors constant, increases in aggregate demand result in higher output, higher employment, and a higher price level. Additionally, decreases in aggregate demand result in less output, less employment, and a lower price level. Governments' and central banks' primary economic policies aim to increase or decrease aggregate demand depending on economic conditions.

How it is used: Recently the Federal Reserve raised interest rates to reduce **aggregate demand**, slowing down inflation.

aggregate production function

positive relationship between an economy's output and the employment of workers while holding other inputs constant

What it is: holding the amount of capital constant, this function shows how an economy's output increases at an increasing and then diminishing rate as more workers are employed

How it works: Assuming a constant amount of physical capital, as workers are hired by firms, an economy's output initially increases at an increasing rate. However, as more workers are added to the same amount of capital, the additional output generated diminishes because the amount of capital per worker is decreasing. This is the aggregate production function, and it increases when labor becomes more productive because either workers have access to more technology or the workers improve their skills or abilities. The aggregate production function determines the amount of output an economy can produce in the long run while fully employing all available labor.

How it is used: Mandatory education, increased technology, and improved healthcare have all contributed to increasing the economy's **aggregate production function**.

business cycle

variations in an economy's output over time

What it is: a period when the economy experiences both increases and decreases in output and employment

How it works: An economy's output changes from year to year depending on different factors; these changes are referred to as a business cycle. Sometimes the economy expands and other times it contracts. The regular expansions and contractions in economic output affect employment and prices and can be severe or mild. Severe contractions are called recessions, which are accompanied by high unemployment, while severe expansions are often referred as bubbles or inflationary gaps and are accompanied by lower-than-normal unemployment and higher inflation. The Great Depression is a notable example of a downturn in the business cycle, while the expansion in 2021 is an example of an upturn in the cycle.

How it is used: When owners and managers see a slowdown in business, they expect that they are entering the contraction phase of the **business cycle**.

circular flow model

simple economic model used to explain spending, income, and output

What it is: a model that shows how households, businesses, governments, and the rest of the world exchange goods and services in exchange for resources

How it works: This model shows the flow of goods and resources in exchange for flows of spending and income between the private, public, and foreign sectors of the economy. Households earn income by selling their resources to businesses and government, and they then spend their income on goods and services produced by business. Additionally, they pay taxes to get benefits from the government. Businesses buy resources like labor from households and capital from other businesses, and they then sell their goods and services to households, other businesses, and the government. Government buys resources from households, purchases goods and services from firms, and collects taxes from both. The circular flow model shows that the value of everything produced in an economy equals the amount spent on buying it in one market, and the income earned in another market from producing the output.

How it is used: A teacher showed her students the **circular flow model** so they could see how income earned from households selling their labor to businesses was then spent by households as they bought goods and services from the businesses.

civilian working-age population

everybody sixteen years and older who can work

What it is: people who can legally enter the labor force and get a job

How it works: Economists interested in the size of a country's labor force must first determine how many people can participate in the labor force. So, they calculate how many people in a country are of legal age to work that are not currently full-time students, in the military, or otherwise institutionalized. The civilian working-age population is the maximum possible size for a country's labor force. The ability of an economy to produce output is dependent on the rate at which this population participates in the labor force. The larger the percentage, the more an economy can potentially produce. The population's size is measured by the US Census Bureau.

How it is used: During times of war, the **civilian working-age population** may decline because military rates rise, and those who join are unable to work elsewhere.

COLA (cost-of-living adjustment)

pay raise tied to the inflation rate

What it is: Social Security and some pensions increase retirees' pay by the rate of inflation so that their cost of living stays the same over time

How it works: When a person stops working and retires on a pension or Social Security, their income remains the same while the price of everything slowly goes up. The result is their standard of living goes down as time passes. Social Security and some pensions include COLA to offset the decline in the standard of living caused by rising prices. For example, if the CPI (consumer price index) increases by 2%, people receiving Social Security benefits will receive a 2% increase in their monthly benefit to maintain the same standard of living. Sometimes employers will pay a COLA to their employees to maintain their workforce and help with morale.

How it is used: Retirees worried about the effects of inflation on their Social Security benefits were relieved when they read that they would be receiving a **COLA**.

consumer confidence

measure of consumers' optimism or pessimism about the economy

What it is: the willingness of consumers to spend or save is influenced by prices and consumers' expectations regarding their job security and future income

How it works: The Conference Board and the University of Michigan both regularly conduct surveys to determine the level of confidence consumers have in the economy. The baseline for confidence is 100, so numbers greater than that reflect consumers are more confident than not that the economy is doing well, so they are more willing to spend their income. When the survey shows a number less than 100, consumers are not as confident and thus less willing to spend their income. Changes in consumer confidence are part of a self-reinforcing feedback loop where confidence begets more confidence and vice versa.

How it is used: Politicians running for re-election are more likely to win when **consumer confidence** in the economy is high.

consumption

household spending on goods and services

What it is: when households satisfy their needs and wants by purchasing goods and services

How it works: Households demand goods and services in the economy, and the spending to get those goods is the act of consumption. For most things, consumption is determined by how much income people have available after paying taxes. Some types of consumption are independent of income, such as spending on basic needs like food, clothing, shelter, and healthcare. Either way, consumption counts for about two-thirds of all spending in the US and is the main determinant of output, employment, and prices in the economy.

How it is used: During the Great Depression, **consumption** decreased dramatically because so many people lost their sources of income.

contraction

decrease in output and employment

What it is: a phase in the business cycle where output and employment decrease over time

How it works: When households, businesses, governments, or the rest of the world spend significantly less, the result may be an economic contraction. Contractions are associated with economic recessions and are marked by decreased business activity and high unemployment. Policymakers try to intervene if a contraction is persistent because the loss of income creates a negative feedback loop, resulting in further decreases in business activity and even higher unemployment.

How it is used: The government boosted spending and decreased income taxes while the central bank lowered their key interest rates to reverse an economic **contraction**.

core inflation

measure of price changes that ignores volatile food and energy prices

What it is: a measure of overall price fluctuations excluding food and energy

How it works: Because food and energy prices can change rapidly, independent of the general health of the economy, policymakers use core inflation when making decisions. They do this so that prices are not influenced by wild swings in the price of oil or food commodities. By focusing on core inflation, which is more stable, economic policymakers can gain a better understanding of what is happening to the average prices consumers must pay for most goods and adjust their policies accordingly.

How it is used: A sudden spike in oil prices drove overall inflation to 3%, but **core inflation** remained stable at 2%, so central bank policymakers made no change to interest rates.

cost-push inflation

increases in product prices caused by high prices in raw materials, labor, or capital

What it is: what happens to the economy when businesses experience increases in the cost of production, forcing them to increase the price of their goods and services

How it works: An economy experiences cost-push inflation when businesses are not able to profitably supply as much output because their costs have increased. Cost-push inflation results when aggregate supply decreases while aggregate demand remains constant. Cost-push inflation results in both higher prices and higher unemployment.

How it is used: In the late 1970s, the US economy experienced **cost-push inflation**, which resulted in double-digit rates of inflation and unemployment.

CPI (consumer price index)

how government measures average cost changes for households

What it is: the government's method for measuring how fast prices are changing in the economy

How it works: The US Bureau of Labor Statistics measures the price of tens of thousands of goods that the typical urban consumer pays for in a year, resulting in the CPI. It then measures changes in those prices year over year to estimate how fast prices are changing in general. Policymakers use changes in the CPI to determine what kind of action (if any) they should take to ensure prices are not rising too fast. In the US, policymakers want the CPI to change at an annual rate of 2% so that inflation is steady.

How it is used: Labor unions look at changes in the **CPI** when negotiating wage increases for their members so that their incomes are adjusted for the economy.

deflation

decrease in the average price level

What it is: what happens to the economy when the average price of goods and services decreases

How it works: Deflation starts when there is a decrease in overall spending in the economy accompanied by decreased income. If government or the central bank does not respond, then it is possible that the economy experiences a long downturn and prices begin to fall. People respond to continually falling prices by holding off on making major purchases, hoping it's cheaper to wait. As people delay purchasing, prices fall even further because firms discount their inventory, slow their production, and fire workers. This all results in even less employment, income, and spending in the economy, which in turn makes prices fall even further. In addition, deflation makes the value of money increase over time, resulting in cash hoarding rather than spending.

How it is used: Beginning in the 1990s, Japan experienced chronic **deflation** that slowed spending and income throughout the first two decades of the twenty-first century.

demand-pull inflation

general increase in prices caused by too much demand for an economy's output

What it is: when an economy experiences too much demand for output caused by excessive spending

How it works: Demand-pull inflation is sparked when peoples' incomes rise more quickly than the production of goods and services. Competition among buyers causes the prices of an economy's output to increase, incentivizing people to spend even more to get what they need or want. The demand-pull inflation becomes even worse if the government spends more or taxes less, or if the central bank lowers interest rates. In those cases, people would have even more money to spend. To make matters worse, all competition for goods and services results in firms paying higher wages to keep and attract workers, further fueling the demand-pull inflation.

How it is used: During the COVID-19 pandemic, the economy experienced **demand-pull inflation** because household incomes increased while the economy's output simultaneously decreased.

discouraged worker

person who has given up on applying for jobs because they do not think there is any work available for them

What it is: a person who does not participate in the labor force because they have given up on submitting applications for employment

How it works: When someone begins applying for work without currently being employed, they are classified as unemployed. However, if the person gives up on applying without having found a job, then they are no longer classified as unemployed. This means that the official unemployment rate may understate joblessness in the economy during a recession as many become discouraged workers. The number of discouraged workers in the US even in an economy with full employment may be as high as half a million people.

How it is used: During the Great Depression, many stopped looking for work and became **discouraged workers**, making the unemployment rate understated.

disinflation

decrease in the rate of inflation

What it is: when the inflation rate drops, for example from 4% to 2%

How it works: When an economy experiences disinflation, or slowed inflation rates, prices are still rising but not as fast as before. Disinflation often results from a country's central bank increasing interest rates to tame inflation. In general, disinflation is good for the economy because it means price increases are slowing—not to be confused with deflation, where prices are falling. From 2022 through 2024, the US economy experienced disinflation where the inflation rate decreased from above 8% to below 3% as output expanded while the central bank maintained higher than normal interest rates.

How it is used: Federal Reserve Chairman Paul Volcker is credited with bringing about **disinflation** in the early 1980s after a period of sustained inflation in the 1970s.

employment

having a job

What it is: a measurement of the number of people in a country who have a job

How it works: As an economy's output grows, it needs more workers to produce the goods and services. Increases in employment, or people with jobs, are directly related to increases in economic output, while decreases in employment result in less output being produced. Higher levels of employment in an economy also correspond to lower levels of homelessness, poverty, crime, and political unrest. Most countries try to maintain high levels of employment. Government measures employment in the economy by looking at business payroll data, census surveys, and new filings for unemployment insurance.

How it is used: As an economy grows it needs more workers, so **employment** increases.

expansion

increase in an economy's output

What it is: the phase of the business cycle where economic output and employment increase over time

How it works: When households, businesses, governments, or the rest of the world spend more, the result may be an economic expansion where output and employment increase. Expansions are associated with economic prosperity and are marked by increased business activity and low unemployment. Policymakers try to intervene if an expansion results in too much inflation, but otherwise expansions are seen as a positive economic outcome.

How it is used: Politicians are pleased to be running for re-election during a prolonged economic **expansion** because they like to take credit for the economic benefits.

expected inflation rate

rate of future price increases anticipated by consumers and investors

What it is: the anticipated rate of future inflation that is generally agreed upon by households, businesses, and governments

How it works: The expected inflation rate is a rate predicted by consumers and investors. The general agreement about what that rate will be is determined by surveys or by examining the price difference between US government bonds and inflation-protected US government bonds of the same maturity, both issued by the Treasury. The central bank tries to anchor the economy's expectations of future inflation by setting a publicly announced target for the inflation rate. If the actual inflation rate being experienced is the same as the expected inflation rate, then the economy is relatively stable and does not require intervention. When the expected inflation rate remains stable, interest rates remain stable, so businesses and consumers can better plan their saving and spending.

How it is used: Investors in the bond market became worried about the value of their portfolios when the **expected inflation rate** increased.

frictional unemployment

period of joblessness associated with voluntary entry into the labor force

What it is: when a person enters the labor force and begins looking for work

How it works: At any point in time, hundreds of thousands of people in the economy are entering or exiting the labor force as they finish school, leave the military, transition from full-time parenting, or retire. The period where new entrants into the labor force are actively seeking employment but are not yet hired represents a period of frictional unemployment. It's frictional because job seekers do not all automatically match up with jobs upon completing applications, and they must complete multiple applications and interviews before getting a job.

How it is used: Every year economists seasonally adjust unemployment figures in late May and early June as thousands of graduates experience **frictional unemployment**.

full employment output

an economy's potential output

What it is: an economy's long-run sustainable level of output

How it works: In the short run, economies experience ups and downs in output, prices, and employment. However, in the long run, there is a level of output in an economy associated with employing as many workers as possible, resulting neither in high inflation nor high unemployment. This "just-right" level of employment results in an economy producing goods and services while remaining economically stable. Full employment output is the end-goal for government and central-bank economic intervention because it balances the problems of high inflation and high unemployment.

How it is used: During 2007–2020, the economy went from high unemployment and decreased output caused by the financial crisis to **full employment output**.

GDP (gross domestic product)

value of an economy's annual output of new goods and services

What it is: an economy's total production of final goods and services in a calendar year within the country, or the total spending on and income earned from the production of an economy's output

How it works: Economists interested in understanding how much an economy produces can measure output in three ways. First, they can calculate the value of what was spent on all the new goods and services the economy produced in a year. Another method is that they can add up all the income earned from producing the new goods and services. Finally, they can measure the value added at each stage of production. GDP is the primary measure used to compare the size of different economies and is key to understanding the level of employment. For example, in 2023 the US economy's GDP was about $27 trillion. This means that $27 trillion was spent and earned producing $27 trillion worth of new goods and services in 2023.

How it is used: During World War II, US economists' calculations of **GDP** helped military leaders determine how many planes, tanks, and ships could be produced for the war effort.

government purchases

public-sector spending on goods and services produced by businesses

What it is: the spending at all levels of government on goods and services produced in the private sector

How it works: When a city buys a new fire engine, the government is purchasing output created by firms in the economy. When calculating how much output an economy creates, economists include the value of any government and other sectors' purchases in the economy. Not all government spending is in the form of government purchases; governments supply households and businesses with transfer payments like Social Security benefits, unemployment compensation, subsidies, or welfare benefits. These types of spending are not associated with output created by businesses, so economists exclude these when calculating government's share of total spending on output in an economy.

How it is used: When a confused economics student's calculation was wrong, their teacher pointed out that they had only included consumption, investment, and net exports, leaving out **government purchases**.

hyperinflation

fast and out-of-control price increases in an economy

What it is: an excessive increase in the average price of goods and services in the economy

How it works: Some small amount of inflation is normal in an economy, but large and uncontrollable inflation, known as hyperinflation, is a serious problem. Hyperinflation is caused when the amount of money being issued in an economy is much greater than the rate at which the economy is growing. The difference in the growth rates of money and the economy means there is more money to buy the same amount of goods, causing prices to rise—sometimes even double in less than a day. In response, poorly governed economies increase the availability of money, boosting prices even further and creating a self-reinforcing feedback loop.

Hyperinflation seriously damages the value of peoples' savings and hinders businesses' ability to plan and produce. Historical examples of hyperinflation include early 1920s Germany, 2000s Zimbabwe, and more recently Venezuela.

How it is used: To prevent **hyperinflation**, modern economies have independent central banks that limit money supply growth.

inflation

general increase in prices

What it is: a sustained boost in overall average prices

How it works: Inflation is an increase in prices that is caused by either too much consumer demand or a shortage of supply. Inflation is then sustained by too much money being issued in the economy. Inflation is normal when it is expected and relatively low. When inflation is unexpectedly high, it causes problems for households and businesses because it redistributes wealth from private savers to those with large debts because interest rates on previously issued loans are not high enough to compensate savers and lenders. Inflation reduces the standards of living for people on fixed incomes and results in widespread poverty if wages can't keep up. Central banks are primarily tasked with keeping inflation low and stable.

How it is used: The Federal Reserve raises interest rates to slow down consumer spending and encourage saving when **inflation** becomes a problem.

inflation rate

speed at which prices on average are increasing

What it is: the amount of change in the average price level

How it works: Economists calculate the inflation rate, or how quickly prices increase, by measuring the cost of a fixed set of items in a metaphorical market basket and then calculating the percentage change in the cost of the basket over time. For example, if the basket cost $1,000 in 2022 and increased to $1,080 in 2023, economists would calculate the inflation rate to be 8% because a change of $80 represents an 8% increase in the cost of the basket from its original amount of $1,000. In the US, normal rates of inflation range from 1.5%–3%.

How it is used: If the **inflation rate** is greater than the rate at which your take-home pay increases, your standard of living decreases.

investment

purchases of new construction, machines, tools, equipment, and unsold inventory

What it is: business spending that results in either increased capital, replacement of worn capital, or new unsold inventory

How it works: Investments involve spending money to better a business; sometimes investments are at a household level and involve buying newly constructed homes. Firms make investments so that they can expand their businesses to produce more output. Plus, firms invest in replacing worn-out equipment that has depreciated. When the investment in physical capital exceeds depreciation, then the economy can eventually grow because workers will become more productive as they have access to more capital. Interest rates are crucial when investing, as businesses must borrow or use savings to finance.

How it is used: A student was surprised to learn that **investment** in economics doesn't apply to putting money into the stock market but is instead about businesses purchasing capital.

labor force

combined number of employed people plus jobless people job searching

What it is: a subset of the larger civilian working-age population that is either actively employed or jobless but actively seeking work

How it works: To be considered as part of the labor force, people must either currently be working at a job or actively completing applications for employment. The size of the labor force is important to economists because this number plus the availability of physical capital in an economy determine how much output an economy can produce. Over time, the size of the labor force (and thus the economy) has grown as the population has grown, but its size has also increased because people who were once prohibited from working due to gender or race are now able to work. In 2023, the US labor force was about 169.5 million people, of which 163.2 million were employed and 6.3 million were unemployed. The working-age population was about 208 million and the total population of the US was about 335 million people, meaning over half of Americans are in the labor force.

How it is used: Some young people choose not to participate in the **labor force**, choosing to go to college instead.

labor force participation rate

percentage of the civilian working-age population that is either working or actively seeking work

What it is: the labor force divided by the civilian working-age population

How it works: The labor force participation rate is an important measure for economists seeking to understand employment and joblessness in a country. During periods of economic expansion, the labor force participation rate generally increases because people choose to work. During economic downturns, the labor force participation rate declines as people exit the labor force due to job scarcity. Since 2000, the labor force participation rate in the US has slowly declined from 67% to 62.7%, as the larger baby boom generation of older workers have slowly exited while the younger and smaller generations of people have delayed entry into the labor force.

How it is used: Yemen has a much lower **labor force participation rate** than Switzerland partially because women in Yemen are barred from many types of employment.

LRAS (long-run aggregate supply)

potential output supplied by all firms in an economy

What it is: the potential output all firms in an economy can produce when fully employing labor and capital independent of changes in prices

How it works: The long run means that the effects of inflation are reflected in the prices of goods and services, as well as the prices of labor and capital that businesses use to produce output. The economy's LRAS is effectively the same as an economy's potential to produce output no matter the price level.

How it is used: An economy experiencing full employment of labor is operating on its **LRAS** curve.

LRPC (long-run Phillips curve)

observation that there is no relationship between inflation and unemployment in the long run

What it is: part of a larger economic model describing the relationships in the short run and long run between the inflation rate and unemployment rate, which shows that in the long run, the unemployment rate in an economy is not affected by inflation

How it works: In the long run, factors other than inflation influence the level of unemployment in the economy. When prices increase, workers demand higher wages to reflect the change in prices and so there is no effect on the unemployment rate because firms cannot afford to hire additional workers. When prices in the economy decrease, workers accept lower wages and again there is no effect on the unemployment rate. The LRPC exists at the rate of unemployment associated with an economy producing its potential output.

How it is used: The **LRPC** implies that government's efforts to spend to alleviate unemployment won't actually impact unemployment and will make things more expensive.

marginally attached worker

person willing and available to work but not currently in the labor force

What it is: a working-age person who has participated in the labor force in the last year and is willing and available to work but is neither currently employed nor actively seeking a job

How it works: Not all jobless people are unemployed. Some people are willing and able to work but have not formally entered the labor force by completing and submitting job applications. These marginally attached workers are not included in the official unemployment statistic because to be unemployed they must not only be jobless but also actively seeking employment. Marginally attached workers may choose to only participate in the labor force for certain parts of the year and then voluntarily exit at other times. The presence of marginally attached workers in the working-age population means that joblessness is underreported by the official unemployment rate.

How it is used: Many retirees are considered **marginally attached workers** because they will do freelance work for additional income, waiting for specific projects to come their way.

misery index

sum of the inflation rate and the unemployment rate

What it is: adding the annual inflation rate to the unemployment rate to measure how people are faring in an economy

How it works: Usually, inflation rates and unemployment rates move in opposite directions. This means that increases in one are offset by decreases in the other and overall economic misery remains rather stable. A misery index adds together inflation and unemployment rates; a value of less than 8 indicates economic conditions are generally favorable with relatively low unemployment and low inflation. Misery index values greater than 8 indicate either one or both rates is creating economic hardship for the average person in the economy. For example, during the Great Depression, the misery index would have been quite high (20+) because of the extremely high unemployment rate at that time. Again, in the early 1980s, the misery index was high (20+) because of a combination of double-digit inflation and unemployment. Most recently, the misery index was relatively high (10+) from 2020 to 2023 because of COVID-19 unemployment and then a high inflation rate.

How it is used: In August 2024, according to Federal Reserve data, the **misery index** was 6.8, because the inflation rate was 2.6% and the unemployment rate was 4.2%.

natural rate of unemployment

normal amount of people without jobs for an economy

What it is: the percentage of people without jobs associated with an economy producing its long-run potential output

How it works: In the absence of downturns in the business cycle, the unemployment rate is made up of people who are voluntarily seeking work and people who are having trouble finding jobs because of a mismatch between their skill sets and the jobs available. These types of unemployment are always present and combine to create the natural rate of unemployment. The idea of the natural rate of unemployment came from the work of Milton Friedman and Edmund Phelps who witnessed the normal trade-off between the unemployment rate and the inflation rate break down during the 1970s. They concluded that the long-term normal unemployment rate for an economy was completely independent of the inflation rate in developing their natural rate hypothesis. The general agreement among economists in the mid 2020s was that the natural rate of unemployment is about 4.5%.

How it is used: In 2024, the Federal Reserve began lowering interest rates as the inflation rate decreased and the unemployment rate trended back up toward its **natural rate of unemployment**.

nominal GDP (gross domestic product)

value of an economy's output at today's prices

What it is: when economists calculate the output of a country using money as the unit of measure

How it works: The nominal GDP is simply economic output at current prices. For example, assume an economy that produces 2 beach balls, 1 ice-cream cone, and 1 tricycle. Taking these products, economists would then measure output using money because it allows them to capture the value of the output in terms we can understand. Assume today's prices are $1 per beach ball, $0.50 per ice-cream cone, and $10 per tricycle. It is now a simple matter of multiplication and then addition to calculate the economy's nominal GDP: (2 beach balls × $1) + (1 ice-cream cone × $0.50) + (1 tricycle × $10) = $12.50.

How it is used: The **nominal GDP** of the US is more than $27 trillion, as there are many products and services offered.

Okun's law

increases in unemployment decrease GDP

What it is: Arthur Okun observed that a 1% increase in the unemployment rate resulted in a 2% decrease in the economy's output in any given year

How it works: It takes labor to produce an economy's output. When fewer laborers are employed, less is produced. This observation allows economists to calculate the dollar cost of unemployment in the economy. Assume that in year 1 the unemployment rate is 5%, and the GDP is $100. If in year 2 the unemployment rate increases to 6% while average labor productivity remains constant, then what is the value of lost output in the economy? In this example, a 1% increase in the unemployment rate would reduce the economy's output by 2% or $2, making year 2's GDP $98. Okun's law implies that there is a real cost to unemployment, and policymakers should consider that cost in making policy decisions that affect the economy.

How it is used: Remembering **Okun's law**, an economic advisor to the president cautioned against an increase in corporate taxes, as the unemployment rate would rise and affect output.

output gap

difference between actual production and potential production in an economy

What it is: whenever the economy experiences economic production greater or less than the efficient level of production

How it works: Over time, the economy experiences ups and downs in actual output relative to potential output, or the sustainable level of production. The dollar value of the resulting differences represents an economy's output gap. For example, assume potential output in an economy is $10 trillion, but actual output is $9.5 trillion. In this case, the output gap is $10 trillion – $9.5 trillion = $500 billion below potential. When an actual output is less than potential output, the economy experiences an output gap referred to as a recessionary gap. When actual output is greater than potential output, the economy experiences something called an inflationary gap. Whether it is a recessionary gap or an inflationary gap, output gaps in general create problems for the economy. In the case of recessionary gaps, the problem is high unemployment, and in the case of inflationary gaps, the problem is high prices.

How it is used: The high unemployment caused by the COVID-19 pandemic shutdown resulted in a large recessionary **output gap**.

PCE (personal consumption expenditure) price index
measure of price changes in the economy

What it is: an index used to measure inflation that looks at a much broader range of purchases by consumers

How it works: The PCE price index shows how costs change in the economy, and is measured differently than the consumer price index (CPI). Where the CPI relies on a fixed market basket approach, the PCE price index better reflects consumers' changing purchasing patterns. Most of the time, the PCE price index and the CPI yield similar results, but because the PCE price index is more inclusive and less volatile, it is preferred by Federal Reserve policymakers. Like other measures of inflation, the PCE price index has different versions such as the core PCE index, which removes more volatile prices (food and energy) from its calculation.

How it is used: The Federal Reserve lowered interest rates today after seeing that the **PCE price index** showed 2% inflation for 2 consecutive months.

peak
end of an economic expansion and the beginning of an economic contraction

What it is: the transition from an expanding economy to a contracting economy

How it works: A result of the business cycle is that the economy goes through phases of expansion and contraction. The end of an economic expansion is called a peak and it is often marked by low rates of unemployment and high rates of inflation or other high asset prices (houses and stocks). Peaks in the business cycle end when either higher wages cause businesses to cut back on production, resulting in less output, or when central banks intervene to lower inflation by raising interest rates. Either way, the peak is followed by an economic contraction where output falls, unemployment rises, and inflation typically decreases.

How it is used: The economy reached a **peak** in 2007 driven by increasing home prices before suffering a severe contraction triggered by the financial crisis.

Phillips curve

concept of a stable trade-off between the inflation rate and the unemployment rate

What it is: a theory that the inflation rate and the rate of unemployment have an inverse relationship

How it works: The New Zealand–born economist A.W. Phillips observed in 1958, using British data, that in years where the rate of wage increases was higher, unemployment decreased, but in years where the rate of increase in wages was smaller, unemployment increased. Later, influential American economists Paul Samuelson and Robert Solow conducted similar research but substituted the wage rate inflation with price inflation. A similar stable relationship was revealed by the research, indicating that in years where the inflation rate was higher, the unemployment rate was lower, but in years where the inflation rate was lower, the unemployment rate was higher. This relationship was used to justify government intervention in the economy to reduce unemployment by creating a known amount of inflation. However, in the 1970s, this relationship broke down because of changing inflationary expectations as the economy experienced simultaneous high inflation and high unemployment thus limiting the original theory's usefulness.

How it is used: Data points for years where inflation is relatively high and unemployment is relatively low are found on the upper left-hand portion of the **Phillips curve**.

potential GDP (gross domestic product)

output an economy can produce in the long run

What it is: in the long run, the amount of output or GDP that can be produced in an economy, as determined by the amount of labor and capital employed and the average productivity of labor

How it works: While output can vary from year to year based on changes in spending in an economy, its long-run ability to produce output is determined by a combination of labor, capital, and productivity. This combination of factors effectively sets a limit on how much output can be produced for a sustained period, or potential GDP. The idea of potential GDP is illustrated in several important models of the economy, including the production possibilities curve, the business cycle, the aggregate production function, and the aggregate demand–aggregate supply model. In each, potential GDP serves as a reference point indicating economic health and stability. Economic policy conducted by the government and the central bank centers around maintaining output at potential GDP while keeping prices stable.

How it is used: The economy experiences recessions when actual output is less than **potential GDP**.

price level

current average prices in an economy

What it is: a unitless number used to compare relative price changes between economics or between different time periods for the same economy

How it works: The US Bureau of Labor Statistics and Bureau of Economic Analysis both produce statistical research about price changes and inflation. In this research they generate index numbers that have no units—these are price levels. In isolation these numbers mean nothing, but when compared over time they indicate on average what is happening with prices in the economy. The rate of change in these price levels is the phenomenon known as inflation. When comparing one economy to another, an economy with a higher price level has a higher cost of living than one with a lower price level.

How it is used: A recent college graduate from California was shocked to discover how much more affordable it was to live in Texas because of its lower **price level**.

rational expectations

people take in all the information available to them when making economic decisions

What it is: people in an economy witness the effects of economic shocks and economic policy, which inform their decisions on working and spending

How it works: Rational expectations theory is based on the idea that people generally understand how the economy works, and they use all available information when making decisions. An important implication of the theory is that attempts by governments and central banks to influence the economy are disrupted by people witnessing the policies and altering their behavior. For example, an attempt by government to stimulate the economy through spending more may be thwarted by people with rational expectations who know that the spending will ultimately result in inflation, so they spend less instead.

How it is used: Bank bailouts after the financial crisis were criticized by **rational expectations** theorists because banks now know that government will rescue them if they make poor economic decisions.

real GDP (gross domestic product)

the value of an economy's output excluding the effects of inflation on prices

What it is: a figure that removes inflation, allowing comparisons of economic output over time

How it works: To get to the figure of real GDP, economists remove the effects of inflation on measures of the economy's output. They divide nominal GDP by a broad measure of inflation called the GDP deflator. Economists do this because prices are always changing and that influences the current value of the GDP. By selecting a base year set of prices and then applying those prices to past and current measurements of nominal GDP, economists can then compare changes in the economy's actual output.

Imagine that you had a scale that measured a pound differently every day. You couldn't rely on the scale to measure weight loss. By holding the value of the pound constant, the scale can then be used properly. Likewise, by holding the value of the currency constant, economists can measure the economy's output over time and know how much it is increasing or decreasing.

How it is used: People use **real GDP** figures to know what is happening to an economy's output over time.

seasonal unemployment

joblessness that changes regularly based on the time of year

What it is: when people who enter the labor force during certain times annually by applying for jobs are counted as unemployed until hired, and then become unemployed again when the work is finished

How it works: Some types of work are seasonal and so unemployment increases for these jobs based on the time of year. For example, prior to the winter holidays, people apply for retail jobs to help pay for the additional holiday expenses. Also, planting and harvesting in the agriculture industry creates an uptick of jobs, and then unemployment afterward. After the specified season, many of these workers are jobless until the next season comes around.

How it is used: Lifeguards often face **seasonal unemployment** after Labor Day as schools start back up and pools close until Memorial Day.

SRAS (short-run aggregate supply)

direct relationship between price level and real output in the short run

What it is: the amount of output that businesses in an economy will produce in direct relation to the economy's price level in the short run

How it works: In the short run, as the price level increases, firms are willing to produce more output because they experience increased profits. Likewise, as the price level falls, firms are less profitable and do not produce as much output. Changes in the SRAS are caused by changes in the cost for firms to produce an additional unit of output. Changes in workers' wages and labor productivity are the primary causes for these cost changes. When wages decrease or labor productivity increases, then firms can produce more at each price level and the SRAS increases. However, when wages increase or labor productivity decreases, then firms produce less at each price level and the SRAS decreases.

How it is used: Increases in workers' wages not accompanied by increases in labor productivity result in a decrease in **SRAS**.

SRPC (short-run Phillips curve)

temporary trade-off between the inflation rate and the unemployment rate

What it is: holding people's expectations of future inflation constant, a temporary trade-off exists between actual inflation and the unemployment rate

How it works: When expectations of future inflation are held constant, changes in spending in the economy result in changes in the inflation and unemployment rates along an SRPC. Increases in spending result in increases in the inflation rate and decreases in the unemployment rate. Similarly, decreases in spending result in decreases in the inflation rate and increases in the unemployment rate.

If people's expectations of future inflation change, the SRPC changes directly. For example, if inflation expectations increase, the SRPC shifts up so that as the unemployment rate rises, the inflation rate rises. When inflation expectations decrease, the SRPC decreases so that at every unemployment rate there is now a lower inflation rate.

How it is used: During the 1970s, the **SRPC** increased as the economy experienced simultaneous increases in both inflation and unemployment rates.

structural unemployment

specific joblessness caused by a mismatch between a worker's skills and the skills needed for jobs in the economy

What it is: a type of joblessness caused by workers not having the proper skills for open jobs

How it works: Whenever employment in the economy requires skills that many workers do not possess, there is structural unemployment. An example of this is if a job requires literate workers, but no workers in the area can read. Structural unemployment is a common feature in the economy as technology is always changing and industries come and go. For example, as artificial intelligence becomes more common, workers who can't use this technology may be structurally unemployed until they learn. Structural unemployment is best solved through training and education of the labor force. The more skills and abilities workers have, the less likely they are to face structural unemployment.

How it is used: Many workers in video rental stores found themselves **structurally unemployed** when streaming video services became the norm.

trough

end of an economic contraction and the beginning of an economic expansion

What it is: the transition from a contracting economy to an expanding economy

How it works: A result of the business cycle is that the economy goes through phases of expansion and contraction. The end of an economic contraction is called a trough, and it is often marked by high rates of unemployment and low rates of inflation. Troughs in the business cycle come to an end when either wages fall because workers are willing to accept them to work, resulting in more output, or when central banks intervene to stimulate employment by lowering interest rates. Either way, the trough is followed by an economic expansion where output rises, unemployment falls, and inflation typically increases.

How it is used: The economy reached a **trough** in 2020 caused by the COVID-19 pandemic recession.

unemployment

joblessness while looking for work

What it is: the state of being jobless but having applied for at least 1 job in the last 4 weeks

How it works: Unemployment is a particular kind of joblessness associated with actively looking for work. As an economy's output grows, it needs more workers to produce the goods and services, so a growing economy typically reduces unemployment. However, unemployment is never zero because people are always entering and exiting the labor force voluntarily. In addition, because of continual changes in technology, some industries become obsolete and those workers are then unemployed until they can find different work. Higher levels of unemployment correspond to higher levels of homelessness, poverty, crime, and political unrest; most countries try to maintain low levels of unemployment. Additionally, government measures unemployment in the economy by looking at business payroll data, census surveys, and new filings for unemployment insurance.

How it is used: The Great Depression was marked by high levels of **unemployment** because so many businesses closed or slowed, and demand for workers was low.

unemployment rate

ratio of jobless people looking for work to the labor force

What it is: the percentage of people in the labor force who do not have a job

How it works: Unemployed people are actively seeking work, and they are added to those already employed to total the available labor force. The unemployment rate is calculated by dividing the number of unemployed people by the number of people in the labor force. The unemployment rate is always greater than zero because people leave their jobs, and technology changes over time. In the US, unemployment rates greater than 5% are associated with economic downturns.

How it is used: Congress passed a stimulus package to get people working again when the **unemployment rate** jumped to 7%.

CHAPTER 7

Money, Financial Institutions, and Financial Markets

If you were to ask a person to describe economics, they would probably tell you that it revolves around money. Although economics is much more than just the study of money, money *is* an important part of the field. Money is what allows us to trade without having to barter. The flow of money through financial institutions and markets has a direct impact on prices, output, and employment in the broader economy. The terms in this chapter will help you to better understand how money, banks, and financial markets work and sometimes don't work. From *acceptability* and *cryptocurrency* to *liquidity trap* and *yield curve*, this chapter will define and describe the terms you need to know to become more knowledgeable and enhance your economic fluency.

acceptability

for something to work as money, people must be willing to take it as payment

What it is: the ability to use something (not always cash or credit) as payment for goods and services

How it works: For something to function as money, people must be willing to accept it as such. This is called acceptability. For example, assume you have a greenish piece of paper with the words *twenty dollars* on it. If people will accept it as payment, it functions as money; but if people laugh or turn you away, it has no value. Sometimes what was once money, is no longer money. Between the 1820s and 1860s there were literally thousands of different currencies floating around the US called dollars. Often, they were only accepted if people were familiar with the bank who issued it. The further away a person was from the bank that issued their currency, the less likely it was to be accepted.

How it is used: Monopoly money is not actually money because it lacks **acceptability**.

bank

business that accepts and secures customers' deposits and makes loans to earn a profit

What it is: a financial institution that attracts customers to deposit their money in exchange for security and interest payments, and then with those deposits makes loans to customers who need to borrow and charges them a higher interest rate than it pays its depositors

How it works: US banks are regulated to ensure that customers' deposits are secure and that banks manage their risks when making loans. Banks are important in an economy because they connect savers with borrowers. People who have more money than they need for spending are rewarded with interest on their savings deposits, and borrowers who need money can borrow from the bank in exchange for interest payments on the amount borrowed. In their absence, savers would have limited opportunities to earn interest on their accumulated wealth, and people with income but not enough wealth would be unable to borrow to buy homes, cars, and college educations.

How it is used: Chelsea deposited her paycheck and applied for a car loan at the **bank**.

bank assets

things a bank owns or controls

What it is: the reserves, loans, government securities, real estate, and other tangible and intangible property owned or controlled by a bank

How it works: Banks and other financial institutions have assets that they can lend to others in exchange for interest payments. The more assets a bank owns, the more loans it can make to generate more interest payments. Reserves, loans, and government securities are the most important for economists to understand how the banking system works to create money. Also, some bank assets can be used as collateral if the bank needs to borrow money. In the US, the largest 100 banks have combined assets approaching $20 trillion.

How it is used: Reserves are considered a **bank asset** because the bank owns the money.

bank balance sheet

statement of a bank's assets, liabilities, and equity

What it is: an accounting statement where all of a bank's assets are listed on the left and all a bank's liabilities plus owner's equity are listed on the right

How it works: The two sides of the bank balance sheet (supplying liabilities, equity, and assets) always equal each other because assets equal liabilities plus owner's equity. Bank balance sheets are useful for understanding how deposits and loans create money, and you can use them to assess the relative health of a bank and its ability to meet its customers' demands for cash. In general, banks pay careful attention to their own and each other's balance sheets.

How it is used: Changes in customer deposits result in changes on both the assets and liabilities columns of a **bank balance sheet**.

bank liabilities

money owed by a bank

What it is: customers' deposits, loans from other banks, or loans from the Federal Reserve are all owed by a financial institution

How it works: Banks and other financial institutions have liabilities, which are other peoples' and institutions' claims against the bank's assets. The more liabilities a bank owes, the more it must pay in interest to others. Customer deposits and interbank loans are the most important liabilities because they let economists see how the banking system works to create money. Bank borrowing in the interbank lending market is a critical piece of the economy because it allows for money to flow from savers to borrowers in different locations.

How it is used: Customers' deposits are considered a **bank liability** because the bank owes the money to the depositors.

bank run

when panicking, bank customers try to withdraw all their money at once

What it is: when bank customers are afraid of bank failure, and they immediately try to withdraw their money

How it works: When a bank's possible financial problems surface, depositors will try to withdraw all their deposits from the bank but soon find that the bank does not have enough cash for that. Bank runs used to be more common, but deposits are now insured by the FDIC. Also, banks are regulated at the state and federal level to ensure they remain stable and well funded. However, even today banks may still face a bank run if customers are unsure of their ability to get to their money. In 2023, Silicon Valley Bank faced a bank run when several large depositors demanded their money because of worries about the bank's future.

How it is used: In the movie *It's a Wonderful Life*, the main character stops a **bank run** at his savings and loan by explaining to his customers why he cannot meet everyone's demands.

bond

a way to borrow money by issuing notes that promise repayment

What it is: a method of borrowing used by businesses and governments where instead of going to a bank, they issue notes that promise the purchaser repayment

How it works: Large institutions like businesses and governments can borrow without having to apply for a bank loan because they can instead issue bonds. These bonds represent a promise by the issuer to pay back the purchaser. Some bonds are sold at face value and offer a fixed rate of interest. Other bonds, called zero coupon bonds, are sold at a discount from their face value and the interest is the difference between the price paid and the face value of the bond. Bonds are exchanged in the bond market and are valued according to the creditworthiness of the issuer. Trustworthy institutions like the US government or large corporations can borrow at relatively low interest rates, while others must pay high interest rates.

How it is used: A company needed to raise money to expand, so they decided to borrow by issuing **bonds** instead of selling shares.

brokerage

financial institution that connects customers with financial markets

What it is: a type of firm that connects savers with different financial markets in exchange for either commissions or management fees

How it works: Like banks, brokerage firms ultimately connect people who want to earn a return on their money with people who need money to expand their business. Unlike banks, brokerages do not offer their customers with a guarantee that their money will be safe from loss. Instead, the brokerage offers shares of stock in corporations, corporate bonds, government bonds, mutual funds, exchange-traded funds, commodities, cryptocurrencies, and financial derivatives as financial investments for customers willing to risk their investment in exchange for higher returns than they can earn by saving their money in a bank. Brokerages profit by charging commissions and management fees to their customers in exchange for their services.

How it is used: A person interested in investing in the stock market must first set up an account with a **brokerage** before they can begin investing.

capital requirement

regulation requiring bank owners to own a certain percentage of the bank's assets outright

What it is: bank regulators requiring banks to have a specific percentage of their assets free from liability

How it works: Banks have an incentive to lend out as much money as they possibly can to earn as much interest as possible. This incentive makes banks vulnerable to taking more risk than they should when making loans with their customers' deposits. Regulators require banks to put up a certain percentage of their owners' money at risk to counter the incentive to make too many risky loans. Capital requirements ensure that banks will have enough money to meet customers' cash demands should some of the bank's loans go into nonpayment or default. Since the financial crisis of 2007–2008, banks' regulators have increased the capital requirements for banks and annually conduct so-called "stress tests" to ensure banks have enough paid in capital from owners to withstand a banking crisis.

How it is used: Regulators required the bank to sell off some of its riskier loans so that it would meet the necessary **capital requirement**.

commodity money

using precious metal or some other desirable good as a form of cash

What it is: when people use a valued good as a form of money

How it works: People use money to make exchanging goods and services easier than is possible with barter. Throughout history, different societies have selected various goods (from precious metals to seashells to salt) that are relatively scarce, durable, portable, and acceptable as means of payment. For example, cigarettes acted as commodity money in prisoner-of-war camps during World War II and in some Eastern European countries during the Cold War. Cigarettes were relatively scarce, held up reasonably well, were easy to transport, and were generally accepted as means of payment by others. Cigarettes could then be traded for other goods in place of money. The problem with commodity money is that it has a competing use other than acting as money.

How it is used: During periods of political unrest, some people stock up on precious metals to use as **commodity money** if their country's government collapses.

common stock

share of ownership in a corporation with voting privileges

What it is: when businesses seeking to expand offer ownership shares in the company to the public in exchange for money

How it works: Common stock offered by a company gives the purchaser a percentage of ownership in that corporation proportional to the number of common stock shares purchased. Each share held gives its owner a vote in selecting the company's board of directors who represent the shareholders' interests. Owners of common stock also have a claim on the corporation's profits and are entitled to a share of those profits in the form of a dividend. If a person owns enough shares in a corporation, they can control the corporation by determining the board of directors. A benefit to owning common stock is limited liability, meaning the only risk is the investor can lose their investment.

How it is used: Along with toys, the kids received shares of **common stock** as Christmas gifts, making them part owners of several corporations.

credit risk

the danger that a lender may lose money because a borrower does not repay

What it is: when banks and bond investors lend money to borrowers knowing that the borrowers may not pay them back

How it works: When banks make loans and when bond investors purchase bonds, they must consider the chances that the borrower may not repay; this is credit risk. If the risk of nonpayment is small, then there's a lower interest rate, but if the borrower is riskier, then the bank or investor earns a higher interest rate to offset nonpayment risk.

Credit risk for companies and governments is assessed by bond rating agencies. Credit risk for individuals is assessed by credit reporting agencies, giving them a credit score. These agencies assess credit risk by looking at debt-to-income ratio, past payment history, length of history, and many other factors. If a borrower is too risky, they may be unable to secure a loan.

How it is used: US government bonds are generally considered among the lowest **credit risk** investments available, meaning they pay low interest rates.

cryptocurrency

nongovernment-issued electronic money that can be used anonymously

What it is: an electronic financial asset whose value is determined by its relative scarcity and the demand for anonymous means of payment free from government control

How it works: Cryptocurrency is an electronic form of money with its value informed by its scarcity. The various cryptocurrencies (like Bitcoin and Ethereum) are sold in exchanges or can be acquired by willingly accepting them as a means of payment. Cryptocurrencies are "mined," meaning multiple computers worldwide compete to confirm the accuracy of sets of transactions in exchange for the cryptocurrency. The primary benefit of cryptocurrency is that it's anonymous because the owner has a "wallet" that only they can access for making and receiving payments.

Mining unfortunately takes large amounts of power to run all the computers involved. Additionally, cryptocurrency allows illegal transactions to happen, making criminal activity harder to trace.

How it is used: People distrustful of governments and central banks prefer **cryptocurrency** because it is anonymous.

derivatives

financial contracts based on stocks, bonds, currencies, commodities, or an index used to offset risk

What it is: deals used by businesses or individuals to offset the risk of holding certain assets or to earn higher returns than from traditional investments

How it works: Derivatives are financial contracts that take the risk of holding certain assets and transfer that risk to an investor looking for higher financial returns. For example, a farmer may contract with a buyer to sell their produce in the future at a price determined today. The risk is then transferred to an investor in the futures market. Someone buys the contract and loses if the future price is lower than the contract price or profits if the future price is higher.

Another derivative called an option allows a purchaser to acquire shares of stock at a predetermined price. The option investor makes a profit if they exercise their option when the stock price is higher than the predetermined price and then immediately sell the stock. In general, derivatives are useful for managing risks, but not always.

How it is used: Financial **derivatives** aren't beginner friendly because they require more knowledge to make a profit.

durability

ability of something being used as money to stand up to regular use

What it is: a form of money's ability to withstand daily use

How it works: Throughout history, people have used a variety of things as money. Something that makes these things useful is that they do not deteriorate quickly—they're durable. For example, metal coins are sturdy and hold up to repeated use for decades, if not centuries. Other things like paper money are less durable and may only last a few years.

How it is used: Using cookies as currency is a bad idea because they're fragile and people will eat them, so they lack **durability**.

equity

ownership free from liability

What it is: the difference between the value of a company's assets and the value of any outstanding liabilities

How it works: Assets minus liabilities equals equity, or the value of assets owned outright on a company's balance sheet. If a company's ownership structure is a sole proprietorship or partnership, then equity is privately held by either the proprietor or the partners. If, however, a company is a corporation, then equity in the company is held by shareholders (owners of stock represented by a board of directors). Shares are also often called equities. The more equity an owner has, the more control they have over the company's assets, and this often translates to a business's net worth.

How it is used: An investor who owned 51% of the corporation's stock had most of the **equity**.

excess reserves

money available for loans at a bank

What it is: money left over in a bank (not held for withdrawals from checking accounts) available for providing loans

How it works: When a customer deposits money into their checking account, a bank's reserves of money increase by the deposit's amount. In a limited reserves banking system, some fixed percentage of the deposit must be set aside to meet cash demand from customers, but the rest of the money, or excess reserves, is available for making loans. For example, assume that banks are required to set aside 10% of customers' deposits. If a customer deposits $100 into their checking account, the bank's reserves increase by $100. Then, $10 or 10% of the $100 must be set aside for customers' cash demands, but the remaining $90 is excess reserves available for lending.

How it is used: The bank used the **excess reserves** they received from Gina's cash deposit to get Andrew a $2,000 loan.

exchange-traded fund

purchasing fund shares to access a diverse group of financial assets

What it is: collections of multiple financial assets like stocks or bonds, which investors can purchase as a portfolio simply by purchasing shares in a stock exchange

How it works: Similar in composition to a mutual fund, an exchange-traded fund purchases a group of a particular set of financial assets, allowing customers to then purchase shares of the fund to invest in the group. For example, BND is an exchange-traded fund that allows customers to invest in the entire bond market with one BND share purchase. Other exchange-traded funds allow customers to purchase entire indexes of stocks, baskets of cryptocurrencies, or precious metals.

A benefit of exchange-traded funds is that customers can purchase a diversified portfolio, minimizing their total risk. Also, unlike a mutual fund, customers can buy and sell their shares in the exchange-traded fund throughout the business day (not just at closing). For most, the only risks are the normal investment risks.

How it is used: Ken purchased an **exchange-traded fund** when he decided he didn't want to invest fully in singular stocks.

gold standard

system of managing the supply of money by ensuring that all currency is backed by gold

What it is: a method of controlling the money supply by setting each unit of currency equal to a fixed amount of gold and allowing people to exchange that currency for the gold

How it works: To have a gold standard, a country must first possess a significant amount of gold. The central bank then issues currency equal to some amount of gold. Once the amounts of gold equal its represented currency, the central bank cannot issue more currency. Gold standards effectively cap the ability of a central bank to issue currency, preventing inflation. However, economic growth not combined with growth in the availability of gold can lead to deflation. Also, new discoveries of gold affect the existing value and thus affect the value of the currency. The US adopted the gold standard in 1900 and completely abandoned it in 1971.

How it is used: L. Frank Baum's book *The Wonderful Wizard of Oz* is sometimes read as an allegory about the **gold standard** and the 1896 presidential election.

government bills, notes, or bonds

government's method of borrowing money

What it is: the US government's way to borrow money to finance its spending in excess of tax revenue

How it works: The US government uses bills, notes, and bonds to borrow money, allowing it to spend more. Bills, notes, and bonds (issued by the US Treasury, so they're called T-bills, T-notes, and T-bonds) all mature at different rates. Bills mature in a year or less, notes mature in 2 to 10 years, and bonds mature in 20 or 30 years. The US Treasury auctions off bills, notes, and bonds on a regular schedule, and investors can purchase them new directly, or they can purchase previously issued ones on the secondary bond market. Investors have the option of holding them until maturity, or they can sell them easily in the bond market. Because bills, notes, and bonds are backed by the US government, they are among the safest investments in the world.

How it is used: An investor seeking to balance risk in their portfolio should consider holding some **government bills, notes, or bonds** as a way of earning interest.

inconvertible fiat

money where the value is determined by the government's assurance the money is worth something and our belief of that

What it is: the idea that money's value is completely dependent on our collective willingness to accept it as payment

How it works: Since 1971, the value of the US dollar has been determined by our collective belief that it is worth something and our willingness to accept it for payment. Inconvertible fiat means that the money is not convertible to a precious metal and its value is based on acceptance. Most world currencies are cheap pieces of paper whose sole value is supported by collective faith that they are worth something. It helps that the government says they are legal tender for all debts public and private, but our faith is where the value comes from.

How it is used: We use **inconvertible fiat** in our economy, rather than lugging around rocks.

inflation risk

the chance that an increase in prices will diminish a bond's worth

What it is: the possibility that a general increase in prices decreases the value of a bond and the purchasing power of a bond's interest payments

How it works: Investors typically see bonds as safe investments, but there are risks involved with investing in bonds. Inflation risk means that though a bond is paying interest, the interest rate might not match the average rate of price increases in the economy. When prices rise at a rate faster than expected, the income stream from any bond you have kept is losing purchasing power quickly. Also, unexpected inflation means that the value of the bond itself is decreasing as the price of everything else is increasing around it.

How it is used: Many retirees living off fixed interest income experienced **inflation risk** firsthand in the early 2020s as unexpectedly high inflation rates reduced their standard of living.

interbank lending

when banks lend and borrow from one another

What it is: an arrangement where banks borrow from other banks when they need money to meet their customers' demands for cash or loans, and banks lend to other banks to earn additional interest income

How it works: Interbank lending occurs domestically and internationally. In the domestic interbank market, banks borrow and lend using their reserves and pay or earn the federal funds rate. In international lending and borrowing, banks typically pay the secured overnight financing rate. Interbank lending is important to the economy because it allows money to flow from one region to another and balances saving and borrowing across the economy. Most people are unaware of interbank lending until it is disrupted, as happened in 2007–2008 during the global financial crisis, because businesses and households are unable to borrow.

How it is used: Economists and other financial experts pay close attention to **interbank lending** as an indicator of the financial system's health.

interest rate risk

changes in current interest rates affect the value of previously issued bonds

What it is: current interest rates increase or decrease, affecting the value of previously issued bonds

How it works: When a bond investor purchases a bond, they do so with the expectation that the bond's value will remain relatively stable and pay a fair return. When interest rates increase, previously issued bonds decrease in value until their interest payments plus the discount on the bonds equals the new higher interest rate. Likewise, when interest rates decrease, previously issued bonds increase in value until their interest payments minus the additional price paid for the bond equal the new lower interest rate. If investors hold bonds to maturity, interest rate risk is unproblematic, but if the investor holds a bond portfolio from which they buy and sell, changes in interest rates affect the value of the portfolio.

How it is used: With increased interest rates in 2022, banks holding large bond portfolios experienced **interest rate risk** as their portfolios quickly diminished in value.

investment bank

financial institution that helps businesses raise money for expansion

What it is: a financial institution that helps businesses and governments raise money to grow by helping businesses put together an IPO (initial public offering) or helping businesses or governments with creating and issuing bonds

How it works: Investment banks help businesses and governments raise money in financial markets and advise businesses and wealthy clients. Oftentimes investment banks are related to commercial banks (even having similar names); however, the two must remain legally separate to comply with government regulations.

Investment bankers expertly create financial products that meet the needs of businesses and governments. For example, investment bankers help local school districts create and issue bonds to finance building new schools. Plus, investment banks connect businesses and governments with large financial markets.

How it is used: Investment banks were shunned during the 2007–2008 crisis because they had created financial products with excessive risks that led to the collapse of several investment banks.

investment portfolio

combination of different financial assets held by an investor

What it is: an assortment of different kinds of shares, funds, and other assets to balance risk and reward

How it works: Financial assets like stocks, bonds, mutual funds, exchange-traded funds, real estate, precious metals, commodities, derivatives, and cryptocurrencies are all risky but can pay off. Investors balance risk and reward by owning a combination of different financial assets according to their unique needs and risk tolerance; this is called an investment portfolio. For example, investors who want to maximize their return on investment while also earning interest and rental income may hold a balanced investment portfolio of stocks, bonds, and real estate. An investor looking for current income without much risk may have an investment portfolio primarily composed of government bonds and government bond exchange-traded funds.

How it is used: It is wise to seek professional advice when putting together your personal **investment portfolio** because your money is at risk.

investment risk

chance an investor may lose all the money they used to buy an asset

What it is: the chance that an investor may lose all the money they spent on purchasing stocks, bonds, or other assets

How it works: With any investment, there comes a risk with holding the investment. Investors seek to maximize their return on the investment while minimizing the risk of owning it. Typically, investments with higher-than-average returns often come with higher-than-average risk that the principal amount invested could be lost. Investors seeking to minimize their exposure to investment risk will often diversify to compensate for the risk by investing in several different assets rather than owning a single asset.

How it is used: The adage "don't put all your eggs in one basket" is good advice for those facing **investment risk**.

IPO (initial public offering)

when corporations raise money to expand their business by issuing shares of stock

What it is: a corporation's way to raise money and expand their business by borrowing or selling shares of ownership in the company by issuing stock

How it works: Corporations can get money needed for their growth in a few ways, such as by waiting and slowly accumulating some of their profits, borrowing money from a bank, or borrowing money by issuing bonds—or, instead, they can sell shares of stock in the corporation through an IPO. The IPO is the first time shares of a corporation's stock are sold in the stock market and how they make money to expand. After the IPO, buying and selling the stock does not fund the corporation but is an exchange of money from one investor to another. The ability of investors to buy and sell shares of stock, however, is what helps create a market for IPOs.

How it is used: Many small businesses find it difficult to hire new employees and acquire capital needed to expand, so they incorporate and hold an **IPO** to raise the money necessary.

legal tender

money that can be lawfully used to satisfy a debt

What it is: the government declares and recognizes government-issued currency to lawfully pay a debt owed

How it works: In an economy, different commodities such as precious metals and cryptocurrency may function as money, but it is the currency issued by the government that is recognized by the courts as the official way to repay a debt. This is legal tender. In the US, dollars are currency used for debt payment. They are legal tender because the government established this through the Legal Tender Act of 1862 and through subsequent court cases.

How it is used: A bank was unwilling to accept cryptocurrency as payment for a loan and instead demanded **legal tender**.

liquidity

ability to be spent

What it is: the ease with which a financial asset is spent

How it works: Financial assets such as bonds or certificates of deposit (CDs) offer savers a way to save and earn higher interest. The catch is that the saver cannot spend the bond or certificate because they lack liquidity. Instead, the bond or CD must be sold or redeemed for cash, which can then in turn be spent. Liquidity comes at a cost for savers and investors. The more liquid a financial asset is, the less likely it is to offer a significant return, so savers and investors sacrifice liquidity to earn a better return on their investment. Because people always need to have the ability to buy things, they should always have money in a checking account or in cash because these offer liquidity when needed.

How it is used: Sometimes people with a great amount of wealth in real estate or other assets need **liquidity** and must borrow money because they do not have enough money in their checking account.

liquidity preference theory

low interest rates mean keeping cash; high rates mean investing in bonds

What it is: people would rather hold cash when interest rates are low and bonds when interest rates are high

How it works: The economist John Maynard Keynes theorized that demand for money in the economy was determined by the willingness of people to either hold cash or interest-bearing bonds as financial assets. When interest rates are low, the opportunity cost of holding cash as a financial asset is also low, so people hold it as an asset. When interest rates are high, the opportunity cost of holding cash increases and people would rather hold interest-bearing bonds instead. These preferences create an inverse relationship between the short-term interest rate and the amount of money demanded in the economy. Central banks can then exploit this relationship by increasing or decreasing the amount of money available to control short-term interest rates.

How it is used: When the interest rate increased from 3% to 5%, investors responded by exchanging their money for bonds, which is predicted by the **liquidity preference theory**.

liquidity trap

money can get stuck in banks when interest rates are 0%

What it is: a limitation of using central bank policy to stimulate a depressed economy is that once the short-term interest rate is 0%, the bank can't change the interest rate to encourage borrowing and spending

How it works: Central banks' ability to control short-term interest rates provides them with a tool for either discouraging or encouraging borrowing and spending. There is no upper limit to interest rates, but there is a lower boundary of 0%. So, when an economy is in recession, the central bank can only reduce the short-term interest rate to 0%. If this does not stimulate borrowing and spending, then the economy experiences a liquidity trap where the central bank cannot act further.

How it is used: The economist John Maynard Keynes argued that because of **liquidity traps**, it is up to the government to deficit spend and restart spending when 0% interest is insufficient in stimulating the economy.

loan

borrowed money

What it is: borrowing money from a bank in order to buy something

How it works: Banks make loans (using money other people have deposited) to people who need more money to buy something they want or need. In exchange, the borrowers pay back the amount borrowed, or principal, plus interest.

People use loans to buy things like houses, cars, or college educations. Businesses use loans to buy things like buildings, tools, and equipment. Banks profit from making loans because they charge an interest rate on the loans greater than the interest rate they pay to their depositors. The ability to get a loan from a bank is constrained by the borrower's future ability to make loan payments, the amount of outstanding debt they already have, and their history of repaying previous loans.

How it is used: It is normal for people to take out a **loan** to buy a house because many people have a hard time saving up the total cost of a home.

loanable funds theory

real interest rates are determined by saving and borrowing

What it is: the theory that the long-term interest rate that results in economic stability comes from the savings in an economy being equal to borrowing in the credit market

How it works: Loanable funds theory states that when the market for savings and borrowing is balanced, the resulting interest rate corresponds to economic stability. According to loanable funds theory (developed by Swedish economist Knut Wicksell), changes in either the supply or demand for loanable funds result in changes in interest rates and in the amount of national savings being invested.

How it is used: According to **loanable funds theory**, increases in capital investment increase demand for loans and thus the real interest rate.

M1

the amount of money available primarily for spending in an economy

What it is: the currency in circulation plus the amount of money deposited in checking and savings accounts

How it works: Economists interested in measuring the money in an economy classify money according to its use. They then add up all the money classified as available for spending to calculate the M1 measure of monetary supply. M1 represents all money in the form of currency in circulation as well as what people have deposited in their checking and savings accounts. The size of M1 varies over time, and if its growth rate exceeds the growth rate of the economy, the economy experiences inflation.

How it is used: The Federal Reserve reported in 2024 that the **M1** was about $18 trillion.

M2

the amount of money available for spending and saving in an economy

What it is: the currency in circulation plus the amount of money deposited in checking and savings accounts plus money deposited in money market mutual funds and CDs

How it works: M2 is measured by economists interested in determining how much money in the economy is available for spending and saving. M2 is a broader measure of the money supply than M1. It's larger because it includes the balances of people's money market mutual funds as well as all the savings in CDs under $100,000. If M2's growth rate increases faster than the economy's growth rate, inflation results.

How it is used: Since 2000, the **M2** has grown by a factor of five and today it is about $20 trillion.

margin loan

borrowed money used to buy shares of stock

What it is: money borrowed from a brokerage firm for buying financial assets, using the assets as collateral for the loan

How it works: Risk-taking investors can borrow money from a brokerage using shares of stock purchased as collateral; these are margin loans. Using margin loans allows investors to earn higher rates of return on their investments than they could otherwise earn only using their own money. The investor borrows money from the brokerage, buys stock, and if the stocks do well, the investor sells them, repays the loan, and keeps the profit. If a stock decreases, they sell at a loss and must make up the difference. Plus, the brokerage benefits from margin loans because they earn interest on the loans, which are secured by shares of stock that the brokerage can sell if the borrower defaults on the loan.

How it is used: An investor used a **margin loan** to buy $10,000 worth of Microsoft shares, and when the shares increased in value to $15,000, the investor sold them, repaid the loan plus interest, and kept the remainder as profit.

medium of exchange

money used to buy goods, services, or resources

What it is: money functioning as a way for people to buy or sell

How it works: Money performs three major functions: medium of exchange, store of value, and unit of account. When money acts as a medium of exchange, people are using it for purchasing the things they need or want. In the absence of money, people must barter (trading one good or service for another), but this inefficient practice relies on the trade partners wanting what the other is offering in exchange. Instead, when money functions as a medium of exchange, it eliminates the need for the people to want specific things from each other.

How it is used: Francisco used money as a **medium of exchange** when he took his $5 bill and bought French fries and a soda at the drive-through.

monetary base

banks' reserves plus currency in circulation

What it is: money in the banks and in circulation

How it works: Banks store money in one of two ways. They either keep it on reserve with the central bank, or they store currency in a bank vault. The monetary base (or Mo) is the basis of the money supply. When banks lend their reserves to people and businesses, the money enters the broader money supply in the form of new bank deposits. Central banks control the broad money supply by changing the monetary base through purchases of government-issued bonds from financial institutions. Plus, they influence a bank's ability to issue loans by paying interest on reserve balances and setting other interest rates that influence banks and other financial institutions.

How it is used: The **monetary base** has increased significantly since 2008 because the Federal Reserve changed the way it conducted monetary policy and introduced trillions of dollars in reserves to the banking system.

money

anything used as a medium of exchange, store of value, or unit of account

What it is: whatever is used to buy and sell things, store value for later use, or to measure how much things are worth

How it works: Money (from paper currency to precious metals) is whatever is used to purchase or sell things, save for later, or determine the worth of something. It has evolved at different times and in different societies as a way for people to exchange goods and services without having to barter. Things that are easily carried, withstand frequent use, and are generally acceptable to other people are features money typically has despite the society in which it developed. Today, money is generally in the form of a digital record of deposits on financial institutions' computers or cash and coins.

How it is used: When Claire offered to bake her dentist a cake in exchange for a teeth cleaning, they refused and asked for **money** as payment instead.

money market

where money is bought and sold

What it is: the place connecting a country's central bank through the banking system with the rest of the economy and where money is exchanged at the equilibrium interest rate

How it works: Central banks supply money through the banking system and everyone else in an economy demands money in the money market. Equilibrium in the money market determines the interest rate that banks pay each other to borrow from one another. The supply of money is determined by the central bank, while the demand for money comes from a combination of households, businesses, and governments who need it as a medium of exchange or store of value. Increases or decreases in the demand for money result in increases or decreases in the equilibrium interest rate respectively. Increases or decreases in the supply of money result in decreases or increases in the equilibrium interest rate respectively.

How it is used: Short-term interest rates are primarily determined in the **money market**.

money multiplier
ratio of M1 or M2 to M0

What it is: the ratio of the amount of money in circulation and in customers' bank deposits to the amount of money banks hold in reserve

How it works: The money multiplier predicts the maximum amount of change in the money supply from a single deposit. For example, if the money multiplier is 10, then new loans of $1,000 can possibly result in a $10,000 increase in the money supply. Likewise, given a money multiplier of 5, an open market purchase of bonds by the Federal Reserve of $50 million can possibly expand the money supply by $250 million. Customers not depositing all their cash or banks holding on to reserves, rather than lending them, limit the money multiplier's effect.

How it is used: If the money supply is $18 trillion and bank reserves are $2 trillion, then the **money multiplier** is 9 ($18 trillion ÷ $2 trillion).

multiple deposit expansion
money created when banks accept deposits and make loans

What it is: the process of money creation resulting from banks accepting customer deposits and then lending the money to other customers, rather than holding on to the deposit as reserves

How it works: When money is deposited into a bank, the bank holds some as a reserve but may lend a portion of it as well. This is called multiple deposit expansion (sometimes called credit expansion). The money lent eventually gets deposited and the money supply, or the amount of currency in circulation plus customers' bank deposits, gets larger. So, new money is created through the ongoing process of banks accepting deposits and then lending the money to somebody else. Multiple deposit expansion is the result of what economists call a fractional reserve banking system.

How it is used: Most of the money we use is not paper currency but is instead checking account balances that ultimately result from **multiple deposit expansion.**

municipal bond

how local governments borrow money

What it is: how states, counties, cities, and school districts borrow currency

How it works: When local governments need to borrow money, they work with investment banks to set up municipal bonds, which they can issue in exchange for money to be used in building roads, bridges, and schools. Before issuing municipal bonds, the government must get the permission of voters through a bond election. If approved, the municipal bonds are issued, and the government receives the necessary funds. Municipal bonds are popular with investors because the US federal government does not tax the interest income payments. For example, an investor with $2 million worth of municipal bonds paying 4% interest would receive tax-free interest payments plus repayments of the principal borrowed per year until the bond matures.

How it is used: Many retirees who want to avoid paying income tax on their interest income invest in **municipal bonds**.

mutual fund

investment offering people an easy way to own a diverse portfolio of financial assets

What it is: an asset where people pool their money and a manager then invests this money in a combination of stocks, bonds, or other financial assets

How it works: When people buy shares in a mutual fund, they are investing in the stocks, bonds, or other financial assets owned by the mutual fund. This makes owning a diverse portfolio as simple as choosing a mutual fund that matches up with the investor's objectives and then purchasing shares of the fund. Some mutual funds are actively managed by a mutual fund manager who charges a fee for their expertise. However, unmanaged index funds seek to match the combination and performance of some known indexes like the S&P 500 or the Russell 2000 and offer low fees. To withdraw money from the fund, the investor must sell their shares and are paid at the end of the day.

How it is used: Instead of trying to perfect a stock portfolio, Flynn purchased shares in a **mutual fund**.

national savings

combination of household, business, government, and foreign savings in a country

What it is: the sum of a country's private, public, and foreign sector savings that are available for capital investment

How it works: People save, businesses retain earnings, governments experience budget surpluses, and inflows of savings from abroad combine to form the national savings. These savings are then used by businesses to invest in factories, technology, and other equipment. The amount of national savings equals the amount of total investment in a country. Changes in national savings result from changes in the behavior of savers and borrowers in the market for savings and loans. Increases in the supply or increased demand for loanable funds result in increases in the amount of national savings, while decreases in the supply or decreased demand for loanable funds result in decreases in the amount of national savings.

How it is used: Although US households save very little compared to other countries, the presence of inflows of savings from abroad have increased the **national savings**.

nominal interest rate

any published interest rates

What it is: the expected risk-free real interest rate plus the expected rate of inflation plus any premium for any additional risk

How it works: Savers and borrowers use interest rates to describe the price earned or paid for the use of money. Any interest rate that is seen at banks or online is typically a nominal interest rate—some risk-free real rate of return savers and lenders want to earn plus the expected rate of inflation plus any additional premium to offset additional risk. For example, the Federal Reserve's published interest rates they use to influence banks, the rates banks charge borrowers for a mortgage or a car loan, or the rates savers can earn on a CD are all nominal interest rates.

How it is used: The **nominal interest rate** on a bond is equal to the risk-free real rate of return lenders want to earn plus premiums for inflation and other risks.

preferred stock

shares of ownership in a corporation that get paid dividends before owners of common stock shares

What it is: an asset that gives the shareholder ownership interest in the company and preference in receiving any distributed profits, but which lacks any voting privilege for the shareholder

How it works: Preferred stock is a way for corporations to raise money without the downsides of debt or diminished control over key corporate decisions. To entice people to buy shares of preferred stock, the corporation gives these shareholders preference in receiving dividends and, should the corporation fail, preference in receiving money for any corporate assets sold. For example, a large corporation started by a family may want the family to retain control over the corporation and may not want to borrow, so they can raise financial capital by issuing shares of preferred stock.

How it is used: Investors interested in eventually taking over a corporation and electing themselves to the board of directors should avoid **preferred stock**.

rate of return

ratio of payments received in the form of dividends or interest to the total investment made by an investor

What it is: when an investor purchases a financial asset they expect that it will return some amount of profit to them every year

How it works: Investments in financial assets are made assuming the investor will be rewarded for doing so. Investors calculate this reward by dividing the annual profit received on the investment by the total amount invested. The higher the rate of return, the more profitable an investment becomes. By comparing the expected rate of return on an investment to the risk-free interest rate earned on savings, investors decide whether to make an investment. If the expected rate of return of an investment is greater than the interest rate they could otherwise earn by saving their money, the investor should make the investment. If the expected rate of return is less than the cost of borrowing or the interest that could have been earned saving the money instead, then the investor shouldn't make the investment.

How it is used: A $100,000 tool that is expected to generate $10,000 of revenue per year generates a 10% annual **rate of return**.

real interest rate

interest rate excluding the effect of inflation

What it is: approximately the nominal interest rate minus the rate of inflation

How it works: To increase someone's standard of living, they must earn an interest rate greater than the rate of inflation. The difference between the stated interest rate on savings or a bond minus the inflation rate represents the real rate of increase in the investor's wealth. If the rate of inflation is greater than expected, then the real interest rate is earned on savings and an investment is less than what was expected. If the rate of inflation is greater than the nominal interest rate, then the real interest rate is negative. For example, a person saving to purchase a home places $10,000 in a one-year CD earning 4% annual interest. If the inflation rate is greater than 4%, then at the end of the year the saver is worse off because the value of their CD did not increase enough to offset inflation.

How it is used: If the nominal interest rate is 7% and expected inflation is 2%, then the expected **real interest rate** is approximately 5%.

required reserve ratio

the fraction of deposits made into checking accounts that banks cannot lend

What it is: bank regulators may require that banks set aside some percentage of the money deposited and not lend it out so that some money is always available

How it works: Prior to 2020, the Federal Reserve required banks to set aside about 10% of the total amount of money deposited into checking accounts and not lend it out. The goal of the required reserve ratio is to ensure banks always have some cash available for customers to withdraw. For example, if the required reserve ratio is 10%, then a customer deposit of $1,000 creates $100 in required reserves that the bank cannot lend. By finding the reciprocal of the required reserve ratio, we can also calculate the maximum possible expansion in loans and the money supply.

How it is used: If the economy experienced severe inflation, the central bank could increase the **required reserve ratio**, so banks would not be able to lend as much money.

required reserves

money in banks that they cannot lend

What it is: money that comes into the bank because of a deposit that must be set aside and not spent

How it works: Banks profit by accepting and securing customer deposits and then lending that money to borrowers with interest. Central banks or bank regulators limit this profit-making ability by requiring banks to set aside some of the reserves and not lend them; these are required reserves. The purpose of required reserves is to ensure banks have money to meet customers' demand for cash.

How it is used: If the required reserve ratio is 20%, then a $100 customer deposit into a checking account creates $20 of **required reserves**.

reserves

the money banks have available for lending and for customers' withdrawals

What it is: a bank asset resulting from accepting customers' deposits

How it works: Reserves can be used by the bank to make loans to other banks or customers; however, some must be kept in the bank for cash withdrawals. Reserves not loaned out can be either stored at the bank in the form of vault cash or deposited with the central bank where the reserves earn interest. Central banks like the Federal Reserve System influence the size and availability of banks' reserves to maintain both price stability and full employment in the economy.

How it is used: In the aftermath of the 2007–2008 financial crisis, many central banks increased banks' **reserves** significantly to ensure that plenty of money was available for lending.

risk of early call (call risk)

risk that a bond will be fully repaid before it matures

What it is: the risk that a bond may be repaid earlier than expected, and that an investor will lose out on further interest payments

How it works: Investing in bonds comes with certain risks like credit risk, interest rate risk, and risk of early call. When the economy's interest rates begin to decrease, bond issuers may choose to issue new bonds at the lower interest rates and use the money to pay off the higher interest bonds. The investors with the higher interest rate bonds get their investment back, but they forfeit any future interest payments and now must invest in bonds with lower interest rates. For example, a school district may refinance bonds issued at 6% interest by issuing new bonds at 4% interest. Those who paid for the 6% interest bonds are repaid, but likely won't find other bonds that are as profitable.

How it is used: A person planning for retirement by investing in bonds should consider the **risk of early call** that may mess with their overall income.

stock

ownership of a corporation

What it is: a way to raise money for starting or expanding a business by selling ownership in a corporation

How it works: Corporations issue stock to raise money for starting or expanding their business. Investors buy stock on a stock exchange because it gives the investor a claim on the company's assets and profits and provides a vote on the corporation's key decisions for each share of stock owned. When corporations earn profits, they may choose to distribute those profits to the owners (stockholders) in the form of dividends per share. An investor interested in controlling a corporation is able to assert control if they purchase enough of the stock to vote in their ideal board of directors.

How it is used: Young people can learn much about investing by buying shares of **stock** in a company they know and understand, then observing it over time.

stock exchange

where corporations can issue shares of stock and people can buy or sell them

What it is: a market where corporations can issue shares to raise money and where investors can buy and sell those shares

How it works: Stock exchanges are specialized businesses providing a place where corporations (with the help of investment banks) can issue shares of stock. Plus, investors represented by brokers can buy or sell shares of listed stocks. The US has the two largest stock exchanges, the New York Stock Exchange (NYSE) and the National Association of Security Dealers Automated Quotations (NASDAQ). These exchanges list shares of stock in most of the major publicly held corporations in the country.

Stock exchanges help to ensure that growing businesses can access funding while providing financial investors a place to easily buy and sell shares of stock.

How it is used: Trevor was unsure of which **stock exchange** his company should be listed on.

store of value

money can be earned now and used later

What it is: money's ability to retain value, so that it does not need to be spent immediately upon receiving it but instead can be saved for later

How it works: If money is durable and relatively scarce, it can be saved and used later to buy things—this depends on interest and inflation rates. When interest rates are low, the opportunity cost of holding on to money is low, so it can reasonably be used as a store of value. But, if interest rates are high, it makes less sense to hold on to that money. Inflation also affects holding money, as it erodes money's value over time; with problematic inflation, people don't usually hold money as a store of value. With deflation, however, people are willing to hold money as a store of value because money's value increases over time.

How it is used: Nora reached into her coat pocket and found a $20 bill she put there the year before and was pleased because her money served as a **store of value**.

unit of account
money is used to measure how much things are worth

What it is: prices are expressed in terms of money

How it works: Money is useful for measuring the relative value of things. In the absence of money available as a unit of account, the value of something would have to be measured using other things. For example, without money, people might determine a material object's value by comparing it to the relative value of another thing, like deciding the value of a car equals one-tenth of a house.

By using money as a unit of account, people can measure their income and the price of goods and services, helping them make better saving and spending decisions. Value is easier to understand when expressed with money. For example, a new car costs $30,000, a house is worth $300,000, or a person's annual income is $65,000.

How it is used: Before money, livestock was often used as a **unit of account** when negotiating trades.

yield curve
relationship between the interest rates on bonds and the length of time it takes for them to mature

What it is: a comparison of short-term bond interest rates with medium- and long-term bond interest rates

How it works: The yield curve shows how interest rates vary because the time to maturity of a bond varies. Typically, the longer it takes for a bond to mature, the higher the interest rate is to compensate investors for making a long-term investment. As a result, a normal yield curve shows that short-term interest rates are lower than medium- and longer-term interest rates. If long-term interest rates increase relative to short-term interest rates, then the yield curve is said to steepen, indicating inflation may be a problem in the future. If, however, short-term interest rates increase and become higher than medium- and long-term interest rates, then the yield curve is inverted; this often predicts a recession in the next couple of years.

How it is used: Many economists predicted a recession would occur in 2023 or 2024 because the **yield curve** inverted when the Federal Reserve raised short-term interest rates.

CHAPTER 8

Policy Economics

People and businesses benefit from economic stability. Governments and central banks both pursue low, stable inflation and full employment of the labor force. These institutions constantly collect data on prices, economic output, and employment. They then use this data to decide on whether to stimulate the economy, leave it alone, or to restrict it. These decisions are collectively referred to as policy economics. Economic policy, however, is not solely based on data being collected; it's also influenced by how decision-makers believe the economy works, and this is influenced by various schools of economic thought.

In this chapter, terms related to policy, decision-making institutions, and schools of economic thought are defined. From the terms *administered interest rates* and *ample reserves* to the differences between neoclassical and neo-Keynesian schools of thought to taxes and transfer payments policy, economics has its own unique vocabulary for describing the process and debates surrounding economic stability and intervention.

administered interest rates

interest rates set by the Federal Reserve

What it is: a combination of three key interest rates to influence the cost of credit in the economy (the discount rate, interest on reserve balances, and the overnight reverse repurchase offering rate) set by the Fed

How it works: Every 6 weeks, the Federal Open Market Committee (the key policy-making body at the Fed) meets to evaluate economic conditions and, if necessary, make changes to administered interest rates.

The discount rate is the administered interest rate banks must pay to borrow directly from the Fed and acts as an upper limit. Interest on reserve balances is the administered interest rate the Fed pays banks on their reserves deposited with the Fed and effectively anchors the federal funds rate, strongly influencing its market rate. Finally, the overnight reverse repurchase offering rate is the lowest of the administered interest rates, which nonbank financial institutions earn when they swap government securities for money with the Fed.

How it is used: In 2024, the Fed started lowering **administered interest rates** because inflation was no longer as much of a problem.

ample reserves

instead of lending all reserves, today's banks maintain large reserve balances

What it is: the banking system's choice to maintain large reserve balances deposited within the Federal Reserve System where they earn interest

How it works: Considering the 2007–2008 financial crisis when banks stopped lending their limited reserves to one another, the banking system now maintains large reserve balances to ensure that there is plenty of money available for lending and customer withdrawals even during financial crises. Ample reserves banking is relatively new and is the result of the Federal Reserve having purchased large amounts of government securities of various maturities both through open market operations and something called quantitative easing immediately after the 2007–2008 financial crisis. Given ample reserves, changes in the supply of reserves do not immediately affect interest rates, so the Federal Reserve now uses its administered interest rates to affect the cost of credit in the economy.

How it is used: The banking system is less likely to experience a financial crisis because there are **ample reserves** in the system.

animal spirits

fear or overconfidence can influence spending in the economy

What it is: the idea that people's and businesses' spending decisions are influenced by both logic and emotion

How it works: Prior to the Great Depression, most economists operated under the assumption that people make rational decisions when it comes to spending, saving, and investing. John Maynard Keynes proposed that people are also influenced by their "animal spirits," or both fear and hubris. When overcome with fear, people stop spending and making investments and instead save or hoard cash, resulting in economic recession. When overcome with hubris, people spend too much or invest recklessly, leading to inflation. The presence of these "animal spirits" means that the economy's ability to self-regulate is imperfect, so it requires government and central bank intervention to operate smoothly.

How it is used: A stock market bubble, like the dot-com bubble of 2000, is often the result of **animal spirits** rather than careful, rational decision-making.

austerity

reduction in government spending and addition in taxes to address budget deficits or government debt

What it is: an economic policy where the government lessens spending and/or increases taxes to reduce government debt

How it works: Governments issue bonds to finance spending greater than their tax revenue. When the total amount of debt becomes an issue for the government, lawmakers may choose to reduce spending and/or increase taxes to pay off some or all the government's debt. Austerity often results in higher levels of unemployment and economic recession. After the financial crisis of 2007–2008, many European governments elected to pursue austerity policies, resulting in prolonged recession and slower economic growth relative to the US. The US instead borrowed heavily to finance even more spending.

How it is used: Argentina recently implemented **austerity** to help reduce its large foreign debt.

Austrian economics

school of thought that promotes free markets and rejects government intervention in the economy

What it is: a way of thinking that emphasizes individual economic freedom as the best path to economic prosperity

How it works: The Austrian school of economic thought is largely a response to the spread of Marxism and socialism in Europe in the early twentieth century. Marxism and socialism both call for more government intervention in the economy to allow economic and political equality. However, Austrian economics argues that governments are inefficient (if not corrupt); any "equality" is actually equality of poverty and loss of both economic and political freedom for everyone. The Austrian school promotes the idea that land and capital owned by individuals and entrepreneurs competing in the market result in a healthier society; wealth may not be evenly distributed but it's better off than in Marxism or socialism. Today, the Austrian school of thought strongly influences US libertarian and Republican arguments against government regulation, taxation, and income redistribution.

How it is used: The conservative Tea Party political movement relied heavily on arguments from **Austrian economics**.

automatic stabilizers

existing government policies that offset the effects of the business cycle without requiring policymakers to react

What it is: government policies such as unemployment compensation and marginal tax rates, which dampen the effects of the business cycle

How it works: Automatic stabilizers are specific government policies that help to offset changes in output, employment, and prices and thus maintain economic stability. During economic contractions, for example, output, employment, and spending decrease and then more people are out of work, unable to spend to pay for the things they need. This can further reduce output, employment, and spending. Unemployment compensation is a stabilizer because having money to spend when jobless helps to offset the current and future effects of otherwise potential spending decreases. It is automatic because unemployment compensation already exists and does not require political reaction when faced with an economic downturn. In another example, marginal tax rates absorb additional income during inflationary periods, meaning that not all income can be spent.

How it is used: The presence of **automatic stabilizers** ensures a government response to sudden changes in employment or prices.

autonomous consumption

necessary household spending that is independent of income

What it is: the spending on necessities that is required regardless of how much income a household earns

How it works: Certain types of spending are discretionary and depend on how much income people earn, while some spending covering basic food, clothing, shelter, and healthcare happen regardless of how much income people earn. People will borrow, take money out of savings, or sell assets to finance their autonomous consumption when they lack income. Government programs like unemployment compensation, Social Security, and welfare ensure that households can engage in autonomous consumption. Because autonomous consumption exists, there is always some base level of spending in any economy.

How it is used: Immediately after the September 11, 2001, terrorist attacks, people stopped shopping for many of the things they wanted, but **autonomous consumption** continued.

average propensity to consume

amount a household spends on items or labor divided by their after-tax income

What it is: the total that households spend on goods and services as a proportion of their disposable income

How it works: People can do one of two things with their disposable, or after-tax, income. Either they can save it, or they can buy goods and services with it. Because people always spend some of their income on necessities, the average propensity to consume is never zero, and it varies depending on income. Lower-income households may spend a larger proportion of their disposable income and thus have a higher average propensity to consume. Higher-income households may spend a smaller proportion of their disposable income, resulting in a lower average propensity to consume.

How it is used: Economists observe that lower-income households have a higher **average propensity to consume** than higher-income households because spending on necessities is a larger share of lower-income households' budgets.

average propensity to save

amount a household saves divided by their after-tax income

What it is: the total that households save as a proportion of their disposable income

How it works: People can either save their disposable (after-tax) income, or they buy goods or services with it. Because people always spend some portion of their income on necessities, the average propensity to save never equals one (or 100%). Average propensity to save varies according to household income. Higher-income households tend to save a larger proportion of their disposable income and thus have a higher average propensity to save. Lower-income households tend to spend a larger proportion of their disposable income; they may even spend over their disposable income by borrowing or pulling money from savings, and thus they have a lower average propensity to save.

How it is used: Economists observe that higher-income households have a higher **average propensity to save** because they spend a smaller portion of their budget on necessities.

BEA (Bureau of Economic Analysis)

government agency that measures and calculates the gross domestic product (GDP) and other economic statistics

What it is: a part of the US Department of Commerce, responsible for measuring and calculating the GDP and certain price indexes and measures of foreign trade

How it works: The BEA is primarily responsible for measuring and calculating the amount of goods and services produced domestically in the current year, or GDP. In addition, the BEA produces an important economic statistic called the PCE price index used by Federal Reserve policymakers as their preferred measure of inflation.

How it is used: Economists in need of data on production rely on the **BEA**.

Beige Book

review of current economic conditions in each Federal Reserve district

What it is: an evaluation of US financial conditions broken down by Federal Reserve district; published by the Federal Reserve 8 times per year

How it works: The Federal Reserve System is divided into 12 districts according to geography. Eight times a year, each district has economists survey financial conditions in their respective district. Each district's commentary is then combined into the Beige Book with data collected by the Federal Reserve, ultimately used by the Federal Open Market Committee to help make decisions about interest rates and influence the economy.

How it is used: Before making any key decisions, the committee at the Federal Reserve reviewed the **Beige Book**.

BLS (Bureau of Labor Statistics)

government agency that measures and calculates labor force statistics as well as inflation

What it is: a part of the US Department of Labor responsible for measuring and calculating the labor force participation rate, the unemployment rate, and the CPI (consumer price index)

How it works: The BLS uses census data as well as data from payroll processors and state offices responsible for unemployment compensation to estimate labor force statistics like the unemployment rate. In addition, the BLS produces an important economic statistic called the CPI, which is used by businesses, governments, and labor unions as a measure of inflation in the economy.

How it is used: Economists in need of data on unemployment rely on the **BLS**.

budget

government's spending plan

What it is: the US government's spending plan based on the president's spending priorities

How it works: Every year, the president and their advisors put together a spending plan for the US government. The plan is then submitted to Congress where it is debated and often amended. In every year since 2000, the amount of government spending has exceeded the collected tax revenue, so the budget is not necessarily a constraint on spending like it would be with a household.

The government's budget is divided into discretionary and nondiscretionary spending. Discretionary spending includes defense, education, social services, transportation, and more. Nondiscretionary spending includes interest payments on the debt and spending on entitlements like Social Security and Medicare. Social Security is the largest component in the federal budget. In 2023, the US government spent $6.1 trillion while collecting $4.44 trillion in taxes.

How it is used: The president submitted a **budget** to Congress that requested $600 billion more in spending than the previous year.

CBO (Congressional Budget Office)

nonpartisan source of economic data for members of Congress

What it is: a US government agency that helps the House and Senate Budget Committees by providing them with useful nonpartisan economic data

How it works: Members of Congress need to know how their policy decisions will affect the federal budget. The CBO was created to provide members of Budget, Ways & Means, and other congressional committees in the House and Senate with nonpartisan, unbiased information regarding budget decisions. Information provided by the CBO is descriptive rather than a prescription of what should be done. Economic data provided by the CBO informs more than just Congress. The data and information provided by the CBO also lets researchers, households, and businesses understand the effects of changes in taxes, transfers, and federal spending on household income as well.

How it is used: A member of Congress went to the **CBO** to get nonpartisan information to help with their vote.

central bank

place where both the government and commercial banks deposit their money and where banks can borrow money

What it is: the bank for the government and other banks that is also in charge of making economic policy

How it works: Central banks accept deposits from the government and the commercial banks in an economy. In addition, the central bank lends money to commercial banks when they are unable to borrow from other commercial banks. Central banks in developed economies are free from most political influence; they also make independent economic policy that promotes stable prices and can promote full employment of the labor force. A few examples of central banks throughout the world are the US Federal

Reserve System, the People's Bank of China, European Central Bank, and the Bank of Japan.

How it is used: The **central bank** raised interest rates because the inflation rate increased.

central bank independence

when the institution in charge of the money supply is not controlled by the government

What it is: the concept that a country's central financial institution should be separate from the government and not subject to political influence

How it works: In most developed economies, the central bank's ability to control the money supply or determine interest rates is not influenced by the government. Politicians want to spend money in the region they represent, and if they could issue currency, then they could spend freely without raising taxes. However, this creates high inflation and makes the economy unstable. To solve this problem, central banks are created and given independence in controlling the money supply and setting interest rates. The result of central bank independence is low and stable inflation over the long term. Because of their independence, central banks are often criticized by politicians who argue that unelected officials at central banks are determining economics that affect policy. Ultimately, however, history shows that central bank independence is beneficial to an economy.

How it is used: A populist candidate for president argued against **central bank independence** because nonelected officials were determining economic policy.

contractionary fiscal policy

government's attempt to reduce inflation

What it is: government policy to slow down price increases in an economy

How it works: Governments concerned about the speed of price increases can raise taxes or decrease government spending to reduce the income that households have for spending. Contractionary fiscal policy works by reducing total spending in the economy, which decreases demand for goods and services, resulting in less inflation. The willingness of government to conduct contractionary fiscal policy depends on how sensitive it is to political pressure. In the US, contractionary fiscal policy is highly unpopular, so government relies on the central bank to do something about inflation.

How it is used: Parliament enacted **contractionary fiscal policy** to reduce inflation.

Council of Economic Advisers

group of economists who advise the US president about economic matters

What it is: a group of three top economists appointed by the president and confirmed by the Senate who are supported by a research staff and who advise the president on domestic and foreign economic issues

How it works: The US president plays an influential role in the economy, but often lacks extensive training in economics. The Council of Economic Advisers was created in 1946 to help the president with economic decisions. The council, supported by its own research staff of economists, can provide objective information regarding any economic concerns with domestic and foreign policy. Every year the council prepares the annual Economic Report of the President, which is available to the public.

How it is used: Before proposing a change in taxes, the president conferred with the **Council of Economic Advisers**.

crowding out

when the government borrows, it competes with businesses for people's savings and results in higher interest rates and less private investment in physical capital

What it is: government borrowing creates extra demand for loanable funds, resulting in higher interest rates and less private capital investment in the economy

How it works: A criticism of government borrowing is that it can result in higher interest rates, which directs savings away from private borrowers and toward the government. As a result, less money is available for businesses to invest in factories, machines, tools, and equipment, reducing the economy's ability to produce in the future.

In the short run, crowding out can also partially offset government efforts to stimulate the economy by discouraging business investments. Central banks can counter the short-run effects of crowding out by increasing the money supply. Capital inflows from abroad can counter the long-run effects of crowding out by increasing the availability of savings in the loanable funds market.

How it is used: Some economists criticize government budget deficits by saying the resulting higher interest rates will result in the **crowding out** of private investment.

debt ceiling

limit on government borrowing set by Congress

What it is: the limit Congress sets on how much government can borrow to limit the growth of the government's debt

How it works: The US government spends more than it earns in tax revenue by borrowing. To limit total borrowed funds, Congress sets an annual debt ceiling; when the debt ceiling is reached, the government must shut down because it has no more money to spend. Congress can avoid government shutdowns by raising the debt ceiling, but this defeats the purpose of the ceiling. The dilemma politicians face is that, when the government shuts down, millions of government employees and Social Security beneficiaries lose their income until Congress can negotiate a new debt ceiling. Then, debt ceilings are nothing but a political nightmare.

How it is used: To avoid a shutdown of the federal government, Congress voted to increase the **debt ceiling**.

debt default

inability or refusal to repay a debt

What it is: many governments have budget deficits that they finance through borrowing, but when the interest payments on the debt become too much, they may refuse to repay the debt

How it works: Governments typically spend more than they earn. So, they borrow through issuing government bonds. Investors buy these bonds, lending money to the government to earn interest. When the interest on the bonds becomes too great, the government may either refuse or become unable to repay. When this happens, the government has committed a debt default. To avoid debt defaults, governments and investors can negotiate lower interest payments or refinance the government debt over a longer term to reduce the amount of annual interest payments. Governments with a history of debt defaults typically must pay higher interest rates to borrow to compensate investors for the additional risk.

How it is used: If the US government continues to experience budget deficits, then eventually it may face a **debt default**.

debt monetization

government borrowing by either printing currency or borrowing directly from the central bank

What it is: one way that governments can borrow money is to just print more money or borrow directly from their central bank

How it works: Debt monetization is printing money to pay for government debts or, if needed, borrowing money directly from the central bank. Debt monetization is a temptation for politicians who have an incentive to spend but who do not like to raise taxes. The problem with debt monetization is that it reduces the value of the currency, which results in inflation where everyone in the economy must pay higher prices. Developed economies avoid debt monetization through central bank independence and by denying the legislature the ability to issue currency.

How it is used: Central banks who lend to the government by directly purchasing newly issued bonds engage in **debt monetization**.

depreciation

expense caused by machines and buildings wearing down over time

What it is: physical capital loses value because it slowly breaks down over time, so businesses and households must spend money to keep them functional

How it works: Machines and buildings must be maintained, repaired, or replaced because they wear out with use. The expense of maintaining, repairing, and replacing worn capital is depreciation, and it is a form of investment. If the money is not spent on depreciation, then the capital eventually ceases to function. For economies to grow, investment in new capital must be accompanied by investments to offset the effects of wear and tear on existing capital. Failure to account for depreciation can result in the economy shrinking over time.

How it is used: One of the challenges facing developing economies is setting aside enough money for **depreciation**.

discount rate

interest rate banks must pay to borrow money directly from the Federal Reserve

What it is: a higher interest rate that banks pay to borrow from the Federal Reserve when unable to borrow from other banks

How it works: When banks need money but are unable to borrow from other banks, then they can borrow directly from the Federal Reserve (the Fed) but must pay the discount rate. The discount rate is the highest of the three interest rates the Fed administers when setting monetary policy. Banks are reluctant to borrow from the Fed because the discount rate is typically higher than the federal funds rate, or the interbank lending rate. This reluctance is also because borrowing directly from the Fed indicates the bank is in financial trouble, which could initiate a bank run or even a bank collapse.

How it is used: Inflation above 2% motivated the Federal Reserve to increase the **discount rate** to discourage bank borrowing and interest-sensitive spending.

disposable income

all households' income minus taxes

What it is: the money households have available for spending on goods and services in the economy

How it works: After paying taxes, the remaining income can be used to pay for households' needs and wants. Increases in disposable income result in more spending in the economy, while decreases in disposable income result in less overall spending. Disposable income is responsive to changes in taxes. If government wants to increase peoples' disposable income, it reduces taxes. If, however, government wants to decrease peoples' disposable income, it increases taxes. US household spending is the largest source of spending in the economy, so changes in disposable income have a large impact.

How it is used: Disposable income in the US increased after the government lowered taxes.

expansionary fiscal policy

government's attempt to reduce unemployment

What it is: government policy to expand employment in an economy by stimulating spending

How it works: Governments concerned about the unemployment rate in an economy can lower taxes or increase government spending and transfer payments to help increase the amount of income households have available for spending, creating more demand for goods and services and then more demand for workers. The government's willingness to conduct expansionary fiscal policy depends on its sensitivity to political pressure. In the US, expansionary fiscal policy is popular, so government is generally willing to do it regardless of economic conditions.

How it is used: The government enacted **expansionary fiscal policy** to offset the effects of high unemployment during the COVID-19 pandemic.

federal (fed) funds rate

interest rates banks charge each other to borrow overnight in the US

What it is: the policy rate in the US at which banks lend and borrow from each other

How it works: Banks lend to and borrow from other banks to make a profit or to access reserves overnight every day. This overnight interest rate is the basis for the other interest rates banks charge customers or pay their depositors. Changes in the overnight interest rate, or federal (fed) funds rate, result in direct changes to interest rates banks pay on savings or charge customers on loans. Because the fed funds rate influences saving and spending in the broader economy, the Federal Reserve administers three other interest rates to influence the fed funds rate and the entire economy.

How it is used: In response to rising inflation, the Federal Reserve targeted a higher **federal funds rate**.

Federal Reserve System

central bank for the US since the early twentieth century

What it is: the US bank for the government and member commercial banks

How it works: The Federal Reserve System (or the Fed) acts as the bank for the US government as well as serving as the banks' bank. The Fed is a combination of privately owned district banks and a government-appointed Board of Governors. On the private sector side, the Fed is divided into 12 separate Federal Reserve District Banks based on geography. These district banks are owned by their respective member commercial banks that deposit their reserves there.

On the public sector side, the Federal Reserve Board of Governors in Washington, DC, led by the Federal Reserve Chairman, are appointed by the president and confirmed by the Senate for fixed terms, freeing them from political influence. They are responsible for regulating member banks and are partially responsible for conducting monetary policy.

How it is used: The **Federal Reserve System** is not swayed by politicians, making it unbiased.

fiscal policy

government's efforts to stabilize the economy

What it is: how the government uses its budget tools of spending and taxes to promote full employment of the labor force or keep prices from rising too fast

How it works: Prior to the Great Depression, the government played a limited role in the US economy. With the Depression and then World War II, the government's role in the economy increased. The Employment Act of 1946 made full employment and economic stability a government concern. Since then, the government has intervened during recessions by increasing spending and transfer payments or reducing taxes. Plus, during periods of inflation, the government has attempted to regulate the rate of price increases by setting legal maximum prices for certain goods and services, reducing spending, or increasing taxes. Overall, economic data reveals that US economic stability has improved since the 1930s.

How it is used: During the recession, the government's **fiscal policy** provided small business loans, and they forbore student loan payments to stimulate spending in the economy.

fiscal policy lag

time delay between an economic disruption and the effects of fiscal policy to be observed in the economy

What it is: whenever there is a significant increase in the unemployment rate or rate of inflation, there is a delay before the effects of a fiscal policy crafted to address the issue is observed

How it works: Lags in fiscal policy are the result of time delays in recognizing economic problems, creating policies to address the problems, and finally implementing the policy solutions. Most economic data is past tense, so recognizing an economic problem takes time, and often when it's recognized, it's already been around for a while. Next, Congress and the executive branch must agree to a solution to the problem. Finally, the proposed solution must have a while to have an observable effect on the economy. Because of lags, fiscal policy cannot be fine-tuned and may exacerbate rather than solve economic problems.

How it is used: Critics of government intervention in the economy say **fiscal policy lag** results in fiscal policy causing more economic problems than it solves.

FOMC (Federal Open Market Committee)
the people who make monetary policy in the US

What it is: the Federal Reserve's Board of Governors and five of the presidents of the Federal Reserve district banks who meet to discuss interest rates and promote employment

How it works: The FOMC is made up of the Board of Governors in Washington, DC, along with some of the 12 Federal Reserve district bank presidents. Eight times a year, the FOMC meets to review economic conditions in the districts and then determine whether the fed funds rate, the key policy rate in the US, should change or remain the same. The FOMC is led by the Federal Reserve Chairman, who acts as the chief spokesperson for the committee. Voting power on the committee belongs to members of the Board of Governors including the chairman as well as the president of the Federal Reserve Bank of New York and 4 of the other 11 district bank presidents, who serve 1-year rotating terms, but all the district bank presidents are present for discussion.

How it is used: Financial investors pay close attention to **FOMC** meetings because stocks and bonds are sensitive to changes in interest rates.

forward guidance
when the FOMC tells people what to expect from future monetary policy

What it is: the FOMC gives people an idea of what to expect about upcoming changes to the federal funds rate

How it works: Prior to the early 2000s, future FOMC decisions about interest rates were closely guarded, creating uncertainty in financial markets. So, the FOMC decided to provide forward guidance regarding changes to the fed funds rate so that financial markets could anticipate future changes. Forward guidance along with release of FOMC minutes is part of the Federal Reserve's efforts to be more transparent about current and future decision-making. FOMC decisions have not created as much volatility in financial markets since implementing forward guidance.

How it is used: Federal Reserve Chairman Jerome Powell provided **forward guidance** regarding possible decreases in the fed funds rate based on slowing inflation.

income velocity of money

rate at which the money supply is used to buy an economy's output at current prices

What it is: an economy's current output divided by its money supply

How it works: Income velocity of money is the speed with which we use money to buy all the goods and services produced in an economy. Increases in economic activity like buying and selling tend to increase income velocity while decreases have an opposite effect. Changes in technology like the invention of the ATM and payment systems like Venmo, Apple Pay, PayPal, and Zelle help people easily exchange money and may increase the income velocity of money.

How it is used: If the economy grows more quickly than the money supply, then **income velocity of money** increases.

inflation target

published inflation rate that central banks try to maintain by changing interest rates

What it is: central banks try to keep the rate of inflation within a certain range as a way of keeping prices stable

How it works: In the twenty-first century, central banks have become more transparent about their policy objectives. One way they do this is by announcing an inflation target that they then try to maintain by either raising, lowering, or maintaining the economy's policy interest rate. For example, the inflation target in the US is 2%. Whenever the inflation rate is greater than 2%, the Federal Open Market Committee (FOMC) takes action to reduce inflation by targeting a higher fed funds rate. When inflation is below 2% and unemployment is increasing, the FOMC targets a lower fed funds rate to stimulate interest-sensitive spending in the economy.

How it is used: The FOMC told the public their **inflation target** before increasing interest rates.

interest on reserve balances

commercial banks get paid interest for keeping money on deposit with their Federal Reserve district bank

What it is: the primary tool of monetary policy; the interest rate banks earn by depositing their reserves with the Federal Reserve (the Fed)

How it works: Prior to the 2007–2008 financial crisis, banks earned no interest on their reserves, so they were incentivized to lend as much as they could to generate a profit. So, banks had very few reserves left if customers wanted to empty their accounts or if the approved loans these banks gave ended badly. In response to the crisis, the Fed purchased government securities held by financial institutions, thereby creating more reserves in the banking system. To keep banks from lending the new reserves, the Fed started paying banks interest on reserve balances to curb lending while maintaining large amounts of reserves in case of a future financial crisis. The Fed raises interest on reserve balances when inflation is a problem and lowers interest on reserve balances when unemployment is high.

How it is used: The FOMC may lower **interest on reserve balances** to encourage lending and spending in the economy.

limited reserves

condition where a banking system has just enough reserves to meet their current liabilities

What it is: when a banking system typically lends any savings that they are not required to hold against customer deposits

How it works: A banking system where banks lend as much of their reserves as possible has limited reserves. When an economy is relatively stable, limited reserves are enough to maintain financial stability. However, when an economy experiences a significant shock, then limited reserves become a problem where banks stop making new loans and some banks and financial institutions fail because they do not have enough money.

How it is used: If changes to the money supply result in changes to interest rates, then the banking system has **limited reserves**.

long run

when changes in workers' wage rates equal the rate of inflation

What it is: businesses pay workers a wage rate that, given sufficient time, changes with the rate of inflation

How it works: In the long run, changes in inflation ultimately have no effect on the willingness of firms to produce output because inflation does not affect the firms' profitability. In the long run, the output produced in an economy is solely a function of labor productivity and the amount of labor and capital employed in the economy. Efforts to increase employment through spending alone will result in inflation in the long run because ultimately output is independent of spending.

How it is used: Classical economists believed that government intervention in the economy was not necessary because spending does not affect the level of production in the **long run**.

marginal propensity to consume

change in consumption created by a change in disposable income

What it is: the portion of every additional dollar earned that is spent

How it works: When people earn an additional dollar, they are likely to save some of it and use the rest for spending. This portion used for spending (or consuming) is the marginal propensity to consume. The economist John Maynard Keynes observed that people likely spend some of their money and concluded that when government increases its spending in the economy or reduces taxes on households, people will use some of that money for spending. This then changes the economy more than just the amount of the government spending or tax decrease.

How it is used: When Helga earned an additional $20, she put $5 in her savings account and spent the rest, so her **marginal propensity to consume** is ($20 − $5) ÷ $20, or 0.75.

marginal propensity to save

change in savings created by a change in disposable income

What it is: the portion of every additional dollar earned that is saved

How it works: When people earn an additional dollar, they save some and spend the rest. The portion used for savings is the marginal propensity to save. The economist John Maynard Keynes observed that people likely save some money and concluded that when government increases its spending in the economy or reduces taxes on households, people save money. This saving then limits the total change to the economy from either increased government spending or decreased taxes.

How it is used: When Pat earned an additional $10, he put $2 in his savings account and spent the rest, so his **marginal propensity to save** is $2 ÷ $10, or 0.2.

monetary equation of exchange

formula that equates the money supply and the rate at which it is used with the economy's current output

What it is: the value of an economy's current output (PQ) is equal to the money supply (M) times the rate at which the money supply is used (V)

How it works: In the equation MV = PQ, V (income velocity) is held constant, and Q (real GDP) is independent of changes in the money supply. So, changes in P (price level) are directly related to changes in M (money supply). In other words, inflation results from increases in the money supply. If the rate of M's growth exceeds the rate at which Q is growing, and V is constant, then the change in P (the inflation rate) is the difference between the two. So, if the money supply is growing at 6% while the economy's real GDP is growing at 2%, then according to the monetary equation of exchange, the economy experiences 4% inflation.

How it is used: An economics student determined that income velocity of money was 2.5 when she divided the nominal GDP of $25 trillion by the money supply of $10 trillion using the **monetary equation of exchange**.

monetary policy

economic policy conducted by the central bank

What it is: the choices by the central bank on how to control the availability of money by influencing interest rates so inflation and unemployment stay low and stable

How it works: Central banks influence the borrowing and saving decisions of businesses and households. By adjusting interest rates the central bank directly administers, they influence the interest rate banks charge each other to borrow money (the policy rate). This then affects the interest rates that businesses and households pay or earn when they borrow or save.

Monetary policy can be accommodative or tight depending on the economic problem. To lower the inflation rate, they tighten monetary policy by increasing their administered interest rates, resulting in a higher policy rate and higher interest rates for borrowers and savers. The borrowers and savers are then less likely to borrow and spend, saving money instead. When people save, less money is in the economy and price increases slow. To decrease the unemployment rate, the central bank does the exact opposite by using monetary policy accommodation.

How it is used: The Federal Reserve used a contractionary **monetary policy** to slow the inflation rate in 2022.

monetary policy lag

time delay in monetary policy

What it is: a significant delay between the recognition of an economic problem and the effects of something used to address the problem

How it works: Data on the economy is primarily historical, so recognition of economic problems like inflation or unemployment is delayed. Changes in the economy's policy rate to address the problem take time to affect the behavior of households and businesses, so there is a significant lag in monetary policy that decision-makers must account for when implementing policy. Because of lags in monetary policy, the central bank generally changes administered interest rates incrementally and then closely monitors changes to the economy. The presence of monetary policy lags implies that there are no quick fixes to the problems of high inflation or high unemployment.

How it is used: Critics of central bank intervention in the economy cite **monetary policy lags** as a source of economic uncertainty that can compound existing problems.

monetary rule

idea that constant growth of money supply helps limit other economic problems

What it is: slow, independent growth of the money supply eliminates the need for discretionary monetary policy

How it works: According to economist Milton Friedman, slow growth of the money supply results in price stability and full employment output. Monetary rule is a response to the Federal Reserve's history of poor monetary policy decisions during the Great Depression in the 1930s and Great Inflation of the 1970s. In both cases, the Federal Reserve conducted monetary policy counter to the objectives of price stability and full employment. Because of monetary policy lags, focusing on inflation failed because it was like trying to hit a moving target using old data, and focusing on unemployment was futile because, according to Friedman's natural rate hypothesis, the natural rate of unemployment is independent of policy. If, instead, the central bank focused on the size and growth of the money supply, then economic stability and growth could be achieved.

How it is used: Critics of Federal Reserve monetary policy use arguments from Milton Friedman's ideas on **monetary rule** to support their positions.

moral hazard

when people or businesses are rescued from bad decisions, more bad decisions occur

What it is: policies protecting people from their own bad decisions only encourage more risk-taking because these people think the government will rescue them

How it works: In economics, moral hazard is an unintended side effect of policies implemented to protect or rescue people and businesses from their mistakes. For example, a moral hazard of helmets and extra padding in football is that players will risk suffering more injuries because they are being protected from some of the physical pain. In the economy, a moral hazard of rescuing banks and financial institutions after they suffered self-inflicted losses during the 2007–2008 financial crisis is that they're now more likely to make more poor decisions and expect government help afterward.

How it is used: Critics of student loan relief say that it creates a **moral hazard** that only encourages more borrowing, and people expect the government to erase the debt.

moral suasion

using arguments and appeals to do something rather than using coercion

What it is: policymakers fighting for and making pleas to households and businesses to influence the economy in addition to policies

How it works: Throughout history, leaders and policymakers have used moral suasion alongside policy to affect the economy. Moral suasion as a tool gets people to recognize their ability to change economic circumstances before policymakers act. For example, President Franklin D. Roosevelt's 1933 inaugural address included the statement "the only thing we have to fear is fear itself," which directly addressed the effects of fear on people's willingness to save and spend. Additionally, Federal Reserve Chairman Jerome Powell used moral suasion by promising the Fed would maintain or increase interest rates, if necessary, until inflation was back to its target rate. These examples are signals to people and businesses that failure to change their economic behavior might result in a policy consequence.

How it is used: Moral suasion is used by the Fed when addressing concerns about overly high prices in the stock market rather than changing interest rates.

multiplier effect

increasing government spending creates a larger increase in total spending in the economy

What it is: increases in government spending or decreases in taxes result in economic output changing by an amount greater than the spending or tax cut

How it works: When the government increases spending or decreases taxes, households and businesses experience more income, resulting in spending in the economy and creating a positive feedback loop, ultimately causing more income and spending. Economist John Maynard Keynes suggested that during periods of economic recession the government should borrow money and spend on projects, and this would create more spending throughout the economy, allowing for increased output and decreased unemployment.

The value of the multiplier can be measured by the change in output because of the change in government spending or taxes. For example, an increase in economic output of $1 trillion because of a $100 billion increase in government spending means the multiplier effect was $1 trillion ÷ $100 billion, or 10.

How it is used: The president proposed $1,500 in stimulus checks for each household during a recession to use the **multiplier effect** to return the economy to full employment.

national debt

money the government owes the owners of government securities

What it is: the accumulation of budget deficits caused by spending more than what the government makes from taxes

How it works: Government spends more than it collects in taxes, which results in a budget deficit. Over time, these deficits accumulate, and the government is faced with a national debt. The national debt is a problem because the government must make interest payments on the debt, and then that money isn't used for other types of spending. For example, the US national debt is greater than the economy's annual output. So, these interest payments burden the US government's budget and taxpayers. If the debt gets too large, the government might make significant spending cuts, raise taxes, or even default on the debt; each is problematic for the economy.

How it is used: The **national debt** in the US in 2023 was equal to $33.17 trillion owed to the owners of Treasury notes, bills, and bonds.

neoclassical economics

theory that consumers and producers selfishly pursuing their desires in markets ultimately results in long-term economic stability

What it is: the theory that economies are stable in the long run, so government and central bank economic intervention ultimately has no long-lasting effect on output or unemployment and only creates inflation

How it works: The neoclassical approach assumes that although consumers and producers make decisions with imperfect information, in the long run they can best coordinate production and consumption in the economy without government intervention. Neoclassical economics is influenced by the earlier classical economists and serves as a source of ideas that still influence economists today.

How it is used: Neoclassical economics couldn't solve the Great Depression because its models do not predict periods of long-lasting unemployment.

neo-Keynesian economics

theory that economies are unstable and require central bank and government intervention

What it is: the theory that economies are unstable because the price of resources can get stuck and lead to persistent unemployment, so central banks and governments must play an active role in the economy to maintain stability

How it works: According to this school of thought, wages and interest rates don't automatically adjust to changes in output and employment, so economies can experience prolonged periods of unemployment if the government and central bank do not intervene. Neo-Keynesian economists combine ideas from John Maynard Keynes with the research of later economists to construct theories and models of the economy that acknowledge the economy's inability to self-regulate. They believe that both monetary and fiscal policy should be used to maintain full employment as the economy continues to grow.

How it is used: Neo-Keynesian economics drives much of our understanding of economic policy.

open market operations

when the Federal Reserve (the Fed) buys or sells bonds to affect reserves in the banking system

What it is: when the Fed buys and sells government bonds with security dealers regularly and this increases or decreases bank reserves

How it works: Buying bonds on the open market introduces new reserves in the banking system. This is because when the Fed buys the government bonds from the security dealer, the Fed deposits new money in the dealer's bank account, increasing reserves in the banking system. On the flip side, selling bonds on the open market removes reserves from the banking system because when the Fed sells the bonds to the security dealer, money is withdrawn from the dealer's bank account and transferred to the Fed's balance sheet, reducing reserves in the banking system.

How it is used: The Fed uses **open market operations** as part of its overall policy to help keep the banking system and the economy stable.

policy rate

interest rate that central banks target to influence the cost of loans in an economy

What it is: the overnight interest rate banks charge for lending to other banks

How it works: The policy rate is the primary short-term interest rate in the economy; it sets a floor on interest rates banks charge on loans. The central bank in a country influences the policy rate by using its administered interest rates (like the interest on reserve balances). When the central bank raises its administered interest rates, the policy rate is likely to increase because banks can earn a higher interest rate than before by not lending and leaving reserves on deposit with the central bank. Lowering administered interest rates reduces the return banks earn on reserves deposited with the central bank, encouraging banks to lend to other banks instead, and this results in more banks supplying reserves, causing the policy rate to decrease.

How it is used: The **policy rate** in the US is called the federal funds rate (or fed funds rate) and is targeted by the Federal Open Market Committee.

short run

when changes in inflation are not reflected in workers' nominal wages

What it is: businesses pay workers a wage rate that may not match changes in the economy's price level

How it works: In the short run, nominal wage rates stay the same even though prices may be changing in the economy. So, changes in inflation influence firms' profitability. If prices are increasing, then firms become more profitable in the short run because their labor costs do not change. If prices are falling, then firms become less profitable. These relationships imply that inflation leads to greater levels of output and employment while deflation leads to lower levels of output and employment in the short run.

How it is used: Most economic policy focuses on addressing changes in prices and employment in the **short run**.

Taylor Rule

equation to determine an economy's current policy rate

What it is: $r = p + 0.5y + 0.5(p - 2) + 2$, where **r** is the policy rate, **p** is the inflation rate, and **y** is the percent deviation between actual and potential output; this assumes the central bank wants to maintain a 2% inflation-adjusted policy rate given 2% inflation

How it works: Economist John Taylor formulated the Taylor Rule as a prescription for targeting the appropriate policy rate given the condition of the economy. When inflation is higher than 2% and there's a positive output gap, the policy rate should increase. When there's a negative output gap or inflation is below 2%, the policy rate should decrease. For example, assume the economy is at full employment (no output gap exists) but inflation is at 4%. The policy rate should be 7%. r = p + 0.5y + 0.5(p − 2) + 2, so r = 4 + 0.5(0) + 0.5(4 − 2) + 2 = 4 + 0 + 1 + 2 = 7%.

How it is used: Economists critical of the Fed's decisions compare the actual policy rate to the **Taylor Rule**'s prescribed policy rate.

transfer payment

money sent to a household or business from the government not expecting anything in return

What it is: a form of income redistribution where the government sends money to a household or a business in exchange for nothing

How it works: Government tries to support lower-income households, people with disabilities, retirees, and certain businesses by sending them payments. Welfare benefits, Social Security, unemployment compensation, and subsidies are all forms of government transfer payments to accomplish certain policy objectives. For example, to encourage the production of more domestic oil and gas, the government may send transfer payments called subsidies to producers. Additionally, people who can't work because of disability or age receive Social Security benefits to purchase the things they need.

How it is used: During the COVID-19 pandemic, most American households received government **transfer payments** to ensure people had enough money for necessities.

CHAPTER 9

International Economics

People around the world trade goods, services, resources, and their savings. It's important to realize that people within the countries (not the countries themselves) trade with one another. For example, it is the consumers in the US who trade with producers in China.

This chapter introduces the terms used to describe the ins and outs of international trade and finance. Included are the various institutions and agreements that play a role in facilitating and regulating international trade and finance. Plus, you'll find terms that describe efforts to limit or even halt trade between people of different nations. The last decade has brought about significant changes to international trade, and our understanding of terms describing these changes is important if we want to understand the evolving world economy.

absolute advantage

ability to produce more, faster, or more efficiently than others

What it is: when a country, firm, or individual is more efficient in producing something

How it works: The ability to produce is determined by the availability of resources and the level of technology. When these factors increase, people can produce more goods and services. Even when the number of available resources is the same between countries, differences in technology may allow one to produce more efficiently than another. This is absolute advantage. For example, assume Italy and Spain have similar amounts of productive resources. If Italy can produce more cars than Spain, then Italy has an absolute advantage in the production of cars.

How it is used: The US has an **absolute advantage** in crude oil production over China.

balance of payments

record of a country's inflows and outflows

What it is: as people in a country trade with people in other countries, the sum of all the flows of money between them is recorded

How it works: The balance of payments compares current international with the flows of savings and capital. Current flows include exports, imports, payments, and income for the factors of production and purely financial transfers. Flows of savings and capital include portfolio investment, foreign direct investment, and official reserves. The balance of payments equals zero when current flows are offset by equal but opposite financial flows. For example, the US has a trade deficit with China because we import more than we export, resulting in a current account deficit. The difference is made up on the capital/financial side of the balance of payments as people in China purchase financial assets like US government securities, which results in a capital/financial surplus.

How it is used: US defense contractor exports of weapons to Ukraine and Japanese businesses' purchases of American companies create changes to the **balance of payments** for all three countries.

balance of trade

net exports

What it is: exports minus imports

How it works: The balance of trade measures the difference in the value of exports and imports for a country. The balance of trade is a deficit if the value of imports exceeds the value of a country's exports. Or, it's a surplus if the value of imports is less than the value of a country's exports. The US has a balance of trade deficit with most major world economies because we tend to import more than we export.

How it is used: Many people are concerned with the US **balance of trade** because it is consistently a deficit.

barrier to trade

something that limits or prevents people in different countries from trading with one another

What it is: when governments limit or prevent trade either purposefully or as a side effect of policies

How it works: Governments affect the willingness of people in their country to trade with people elsewhere through taxes, subsidies, limits, or bans on trade. Taxes on trade make foreign-produced goods more expensive for domestic consumers, making imports less attractive. Subsidies on domestically produced goods can result in producers exporting at lower prices than foreign competition. Limits on trade restrict the number of imports coming into a country. Barriers to trade prevent trade between people in different countries and may be used by governments to punish another country's government.

How it is used: Near the end of World War II, representatives from different countries met to discuss how to reduce and even eliminate **barriers to trade** at the Bretton Woods Conference.

BRI (Belt and Road Initiative)

Chinese effort to expand markets for its products and influence other countries

What it is: the Chinese government's ongoing effort to finance improvements in other countries' roads, bridges, and other infrastructure, ultimately increasing China's global influence both economically and politically

How it works: Over the last decade, the Chinese government has financed infrastructure projects like roads, bridges, dams, and railways worldwide. The BRI is sometimes referred to as the New Silk Road, which references the trade route that connected China, Southwest Asia, and Europe in the Middle Ages and led to increased trade between countries. The goal of BRI is to increase Chinese connection with other countries' economies and to develop markets for Chinese-made goods. However, other countries are borrowing heavily from China, making these countries vulnerable to Chinese political influence.

How it is used: People in the developing world benefit from the **BRI** by having access to new roads and telecommunications.

BRICS (Brazil, Russia, India, China, and South Africa)

economic cooperation between Brazil, Russia, India, China, and South Africa

What it is: a collection of countries banded together to form an economic alliance to counterbalance the economic influence of the G7 countries

How it works: Initially, the BRICS grouping was identified by a Goldman Sachs financial expert as a group of countries that promised greater growth potential than existing developed economies. Since, the BRICS countries have adopted the title and now formally work together both economically and politically. Over time, BRICS have added member states Egypt, Ethiopia, Iran, Saudi Arabia, and the United Arab Emirates. The BRICS nations already share a development bank and are in the process of developing other financial systems and structures as alternatives to the International Monetary Fund, the World Bank, and other economic initiatives associated with the G7 (US, Germany, Japan, UK, France, Italy, and Canada). Currently, the economic output of BRICS is about the same as that of the US.

How it is used: Some economists speculate that the **BRICS** group will become the dominant economic organization of the twenty-first century.

capital controls

regulations on the flows of international savings and foreign ownership of businesses in a country

What it is: when countries want to limit foreign influence and insulate an economy from sudden capital inflows or outflows

How it works: Capital controls limit the ability of savings to flow into and out of a country. In addition, capital controls effectively limit the ability of foreign investors to own a country's businesses or other assets. Governments concerned about a sudden withdrawal of financial assets from their country initiate capital controls. For example, Russia instituted capital controls to keep wealthy Russians from removing their accumulated savings out of Russia in response to the invasion of Ukraine and subsequent economic sanctions from the West.

How it is used: During the Asian Financial Crisis of 1997, India saw less of an impact on their currency than did other developing Asian economies because they had **capital controls** in place.

capital flows

inflows and outflows of savings to and from a country

What it is: financial investors seeking higher rates of return or security move their money from one country to another

How it works: Investors and savers are always looking for a way to increase their returns on investment. If a country offers higher returns because of growth or higher interest rates, then savings flow from countries with lower rates of return to the countries with higher rates of return. When savings flow out of a country it is called a capital outflow. When savings flow into a country it is called a capital inflow. The difference between capital inflows and capital outflows is considered net capital flows and is recorded in a country's balance of payments under the capital/financial account.

How it is used: Capital flows between smaller economies and larger economies can result in big changes in the amount of money available for investment in smaller economies.

capital/financial account

record of a country's capital inflows and capital outflows

What it is: the sum of net portfolio investment, net foreign direct investment, and net official reserves that take place in their balance of payments

How it works: Flows of savings, borrowing, real estate investment, and direct ownership of firms are classified as transactions that take place in an economy's capital/financial account. Transactions that occur in a country's capital/financial account represent changes in ownership of a country's real and financial assets. For example, the French purchase of an American corporation represents an increase in the US capital/financial account.

How it is used: Small purchases of stock in foreign corporations is recorded as portfolio investment in those countries' **capital/financial accounts**.

comparative advantage

aptitude to make something at a lower opportunity cost

What it is: a country, firm, or person's ability to produce a good or service at a lower opportunity cost

How it works: Economists calculate opportunity costs of production by measuring the amount of one good sacrificed when another good is produced. When an economy can produce a good or service at a lower opportunity cost, they enjoy a comparative advantage in production of that good and should specialize in producing and trading it for other goods. David Ricardo's principle of comparative advantage as a basis for trade, proposed in the nineteenth century, is now the basic principle behind much of today's international trade.

How it is used: Students often confuse the two types of advantage, but if they can recall that **comparative advantage** means lower opportunity cost, then they can distinguish it from absolute advantage.

currency speculation

buying and selling currency to make a profit

What it is: investors using their knowledge of international macroeconomics and foreign exchange markets to profit from the buying and selling of currency

How it works: Speculators look for profit from buying a currency at a low price and then reselling for more. For example, a speculator may purchase $1 million worth of Japanese yen, betting that the Bank of Japan will soon increase interest rates relative to US interest rates and increase the yen's exchange rate relative to the dollar.

Currency speculation is generally a risky proposition because foreign exchange markets are very large and move fast, meaning profit opportunities are short-lived; millions of investors compete to bid up the exchange rate and eliminate profit potential. A benefit of speculation is the presence of speculators in currency markets helps the markets function more efficiently because there is always someone willing to take on risk by buying or selling currency at various prices or exchange rates.

How it is used: Risk-averse investors should avoid **currency speculation**.

current account

account in a country's balance of payments where net exports, net payments for the factors of production, and net transfers are recorded

What it is: a part of a country's balance of payments that includes trade in goods and services, resources, or simple transfers of money

How it works: Economists classify international transactions into two main accounts in a country's balance of payments. While the capital/financial account is a record of exchanges in the ownership of real and financial assets, the current account is a record of exchanges in goods, services, resources, and simple transfers of money. The current account is in surplus when the sum of net exports, net foreign factor income, and net transfers is positive, while it is in deficit when the sum is negative. The current account balance is a key economic indicator because it shows whether an economy is a net lender or net borrower with the rest of the world.

How it is used: Current account deficits must be financed by borrowing from other countries.

embargo
ban on trade

What it is: countries looking to punish other countries may prohibit trade

How it works: Governments can forbid trade between the consumers and producers in their country and the consumers and producers in another country. Embargoes are a form of economic punishment used to bring about a political goal. For example, after the Cuban Missile Crisis in 1962, the US government placed an embargo against Cuba that prohibited American and Cuban trade. Embargoes create losses on both sides and are generally viewed by economists as bad for everyone involved.

How it is used: When the US placed an **embargo** on Cuban goods, it became illegal for Americans to possess Cuban cigars.

EU (European Union)
combination of many European countries into one economy

What it is: a union linking most of the countries in Europe into a single economy

How it works: To become more competitive in the world economy, most of the countries in Europe agreed to work together as a single economic unit. This union began as economic cooperation between coal- and steel-producing countries in post–World War II Western Europe. By 1993, the EU evolved into a single common market where goods, services, labor, and money were free to move from one member country to another without facing restrictions, just like how goods, services, labor, and money move from state to state in the US. Today, the EU is made up of 27 European nations and is governed by the European Parliament, European Council, Council of the European Union, and the European Commission.

How it is used: The **EU** is the world's third-largest economy after the US and China.

eurozone

group of countries who have a common currency

What it is: the 20 out of the 27 member states of the European Union (EU) who share a common currency called the euro

How it works: The eurozone is comprised of the 20 member states in the EU who share a common currency. The benefit of sharing a common currency is that trade between these member states can be conducted without any currency exchange. However, these countries have no control over the currency or interest rates. The common currency, the euro, is managed by the European Central Bank, or ECB, in Frankfurt, Germany. The ECB conducts monetary policy for the entire eurozone, giving power over eurozone member states' economies.

How it is used: Tourists visiting the **eurozone** enjoy the benefit of not having to constantly switch currencies because all the countries use the euro.

exchange rate

price of a currency

What it is: the value of a currency expressed in terms of another currency

How it works: When people from different countries (using different currencies) want to trade, they must first exchange one currency for another. The number of dollars it takes to buy a euro is an example of an exchange rate. For example, if an American manufacturer wants to purchase a machine from Germany, they must first exchange dollars ($) for euros (€). If the exchange rate is $1.12/€1.00, then a German machine that sells for €1,000.00 is $1,120.00.

How it is used: An American family planning a visit to Japan was dismayed when the **exchange rate** for the yen (¥) appreciated (increased) from ¥144/$1.00 to ¥150/$1.00 because everything would now be more expensive in Japan.

export

domestic good or service sold abroad

What it is: selling a good or service produced domestically to a consumer in another country

How it works: People trade to get what they want or need; sometimes people trade with people in other countries to do this. When a good is produced in one country and is then sold to a buyer in another country it is called an export. Exports allow producers to profit by selling in markets other than their own country. Exports create inflows of money to a country from abroad, and when the exports are greater than imports, the country experiences a balance of trade surplus.

How it is used: Hollywood movies are one of America's most popular **exports**.

fixed exchange rate

constant price for one currency in terms of another

What it is: changes in the supply or demand for a currency do not affect its price

How it works: Producers benefit from exporting their goods to people in other countries. When an economy relies on exports to help develop and grow, they will sometimes create a fixed exchange rate so that the price of their exports remains competitive. By exchanging their currency and buying the other country's bonds, the exporting country offsets the effects of increased demand for their currency and thus creates a fixed exchange rate. Countries with balance of trade deficits, like the US, do not like when other countries fix their exchange rate because it becomes harder for their producers to compete with the foreign producers based on price.

How it is used: Prior to 2006, China maintained a **fixed exchange rate** for their currency, the yuan relative to the US dollar.

foreign exchange market

where people buy and sell currency from different economies

What it is: a market that connects people from separate economies who need to trade their currencies

How it works: International trade requires people to trade currencies as well. The foreign exchange market is where people trade dollars for euros, or yen for pounds, for example. People trade in the foreign exchange market to get the currency they need to then buy goods, services, resources, or financial assets from other countries. The foreign exchange market is so large that over $1 trillion in exchanges are made in a day. About 80% of exchanges made in the market involve the US dollar being traded for some other currency.

How it is used: Floyd bought rupees in the **foreign exchange market** for his business trip to India.

free-floating exchange rate

price of a currency varies based on changes in supply or demand for it

What it is: the currency prices of countries that do not manage the exchange rate for their currency

How it works: Changes in supply or demand for a currency should result in changes in the currency's price or exchange rate. Free-floating exchange rates result when countries do not try to control the exchange rate, letting it come from changes in supply or demand in the foreign exchange market. When exchange rates are allowed to float, the central bank can focus on using interest rates to influence the domestic economy. The decision between having a fixed exchange rate or a free-floating exchange rate is the result of a country's economic priorities.

How it is used: The value of the US dollar changes daily because the dollar has a **free-floating exchange rate**.

free trade

international trade without restrictions

What it is: the absence of taxes, subsidies, and restrictions on trade in goods and services between countries

How it works: Wealth in an economy increases when people are allowed to trade freely with one another. The same is true when people from different economies are allowed to trade freely. After World War II, governments began to reduce tariffs and quotas, resulting in increases in international trade and standards of living in these countries.

How it is used: Free trade can be controversial; when foreign industries are more competitive than domestic industries, workers and businesses in these industries suffer as the domestic economy adapts.

G7 (Group of Seven)

economic and political cooperation between Canada, France, Germany, Italy, Japan, the UK, and the US plus the European Union

What it is: the heads of state and the finance ministers from certain advanced economies meet annually to coordinate their economic and political efforts

How it works: Every year, the leaders of the largest seven advanced economies (plus the leaders of the EU) meet in the G7 summit to discuss and coordinate economic and political initiatives. The G7 and its summit have no formal authority, but it's a high-profile opportunity for the leaders of the world's advanced economies to discuss and cooperate against the world's problems. Leadership of the G7 rotates annually and determines the host country for the G7 summit. Today, the influence of the G7 faces competition from the BRICS—a similar organization composed of some of the world's largest emerging economies.

How it is used: The US president, the prime minister of Japan, and German chancellor met during a side-meeting at the **G7** summit to discuss issues with the automobile industry.

IMF (International Monetary Fund)

bank for countries who need financial help

What it is: an agency of the United Nations responsible for a variety of economic tasks

How it works: The IMF, headquartered in Washington, DC, was originally created after World War II to oversee exchange rates. After 1971, it began focusing on facilitating international trade, lending money to countries with balance of payments issues, and providing policy advice for the borrowers. The IMF is funded through contributions based on a quota system. The US government is the largest contributor to the IMF followed by the other G7 countries. Today, Argentina is the IMF's largest recipient of financial support.

How it is used: When Greece suffered a debt crisis, the **IMF** helped by providing new loans and economic advice to the Greek government.

import

domestic buying of a foreign good or service

What it is: the purchase of a foreign-produced good or service in the domestic economy

How it works: People trade to get what they want or need; sometimes people trade with people in other countries to do this. When a good is produced in one country and is then purchased by someone in another country, it's an import to the buyer's country. Imports allow consumers to benefit from buying from foreign markets. Imports create outflows of money from a country to economies abroad, and when the imports are greater than exports, the country experiences a balance of trade deficit.

How it is used: Korean-made cars are a popular **import** in the US.

interest rate parity

the cost of borrowing or benefit of saving is the same for two countries

What it is: including exchange rate differences, two countries have the same interest rate and there's no long-run incentive for further inflows or outflows of savings

How it works: Savings flow from country to country as savers and investors seek higher rates of return. If a country's interest rate is effectively higher than another's, controlling for exchange rate differences, the country with the higher rate will save. Their interest rate may fall, eventually equaling the other country's; then, interest rate parity is experienced. For example, if the real interest rate in Canada is 5% and in the US it's 3%, savings will flow to Canada, increasing the exchange rate of the Canadian dollar relative to the US dollar, while also reducing the real interest rate in Canada. Once the return on savings in Canada (accounting for the exchange rate difference) is the same as it is in the US, then the two countries have interest rate parity.

How it is used: Interest rate parity forces central banks to coordinate their policy changes to prevent sudden outflows of savings.

law of one price

the price of a tradeable good or asset should be the same in different countries when using a common currency

What it is: easily imported and exported financial assets or goods should cost the same everywhere, excluding the effects of sales taxes or tariffs, when using the same currency

How it works: The price of a tradeable good or financial asset should cost the same amount no matter where it is purchased. For example, if a pair of shoes cost $50 in the US, then that same pair of shoes should cost $50 in France. Likewise, the price of stock shares in a corporation should be the same worldwide when holding the currency used constant. Even when using different currencies, the law of one price applies. If the exchange rate is $1.18/€1.00, then the $50 pair of shoes in the US should cost €42.37 in France.

How it is used: Because of the **law of one price**, tourists should expect the cost of common tradeable goods to be about the same no matter where they travel.

mercantilism

growing an economy by maximizing exports and simultaneously protecting the economy from foreign competition

What it is: an economic system prevalent before the eighteenth century where countries would export as much as they could while importing as little as possible

How it works: Countries that adopted mercantilism focused on trying to sell manufactured goods to other countries in exchange for gold or silver. They avoided importing other manufactured goods and instead would purchase raw materials in exchange for manufactured goods, rather than giving up gold or silver. The idea was to maximize holdings of gold and silver, develop and maintain a manufacturing-based economy, and be self-sufficient. Mercantilism resulted in major conflicts between countries and was eventually replaced with market-based economics.

How it is used: The ideas of **mercantilism** are still seen today in countries like China, which capitalize on exporting and limit importing, focusing on primarily raw materials.

OPEC (Organization of Petroleum Exporting Countries)

cartel of major oil-producing countries

What it is: a cartel of some of the world's lowest-cost crude oil–producing countries

How it works: The OPEC cartel's member states are among the world's lowest-cost oil producers, so they can offer crude oil for sale at lower prices than the US, Canada, or Russia. The cartel countries (like Algeria, Congo, Iran, Libya, and others) use this advantage to limit production by setting production quotas for each member state. By limiting production, they can charge a higher price for the crude oil sold in the world market. Then, countries outside of OPEC aren't willing to sell oil at a lower price, and OPEC sets the world price of oil. To keep their own member states from cheating on their quotas, Saudi Arabia (the world's cheapest oil producer) will increase production and sell oil cheaply to punish any greedy members.

How it is used: Before **OPEC** became the price leader in crude oil in 1972, the Texas Railroad Commission was able to set the world price of crude oil.

policy trilemma

a country's central bank is restricted in its power

What it is: the central bank's inability to simultaneously conduct monetary policy, control the flow of capital, and fix the exchange rate

How it works: The ability of central banks to set interest rates and control the money supply in a country gives them certain powers. Among those is the power to use monetary policy to stabilize their economy, to influence the inflows and outflows of savings, and to hold the exchange rate constant. However, a policy trilemma exists where the central bank can only do two of these at any one time because doing any two is mutually exclusive to accomplishing the third. For example, if a country's central bank focuses on fixing the exchange rate and conducting monetary policy to stabilize the economy, they can't control the flow of financial capital in and out of the country.

How it is used: Because of the **policy trilemma**, the US Fed's power is restricted.

purchasing power parity

way of calculating an economy's output based on what people can afford to buy in the economy using their currency

What it is: instead of using the foreign exchange value of the currency to measure an economy's output, economists also consider what a unit of the currency can buy in a country as a basis for comparing output

How it works: Economists compare economic output for different countries by either converting the value of the economy's output using the current exchange rate or by looking at what it costs for people in an economy to purchase a fixed basket of goods using their currency. For example, economists can compare the size of the US economy to the Chinese economy by taking China's output measured in their currency (the yuan) and converting that amount to US dollars at the current exchange rate, but this way ignores the differences in purchasing power between the two countries. Instead, by using a fixed basket of goods (like food, clothing, and shelter) and then measuring how much of the currency it takes to buy that basket in each country and using that as a basis for comparison, economists calculate output considering purchasing power.

How it is used: Calculating output using **purchasing power parity** and then dividing by the population gives economists a better understanding of standards of living in an economy than by using current exchange rates.

quota

limit on imports

What it is: when governments interested in protecting domestic industries from foreign competition control the number of imports of certain goods coming into a country

How it works: Governments can limit the number of imports by issuing import quotas. For example, if the US government wanted to restrict the number of German cars being imported into the country, the government can limit how many German cars in American warehouses can be released for sale during a specific period. Once the quota is reached, no more of the German cars can be released, and they must remain in the warehouse until the next period.

How it is used: During the 1980s, American automobile manufacturers and workers' unions called for **quotas** on foreign cars to help protect the domestic car industry.

tariff

tax on imports

What it is: when governments interested in protecting domestic industries from foreign competition place a tax on imports, making them more expensive

How it works: Manufacturers and workers seeking to protect their industry from foreign competition ask for government to protect them by taxing imports. The tax on imports, or tariff, makes the foreign good relatively more expensive, allowing the domestically produced goods to be competitively priced. With tariffs, consumers pay the price because this tax makes the imports and domestic goods more expensive because there is the same amount of demand with less supply. Economists generally agree that tariffs are bad for economies because they result in a loss of consumer surplus. Also, countries facing tariffs on their exports often retaliate by placing tariffs on imports to their country, resulting in less trade and higher prices all around.

How it is used: The US placed a 100% **tariff** on electric vehicles manufactured in China to protect domestic electric carmakers.

USMCA (The US-Mexico-Canada Agreement)

trade agreement between the countries in North America

What it is: a 2020 trade agreement between the US, Mexico, and Canada that replaced the North American Free Trade Agreement (NAFTA)

How it works: USMCA is a free-trade agreement that allows people in North America to trade with few restrictions. Before USMCA, the three countries traded under NAFTA. By removing restrictions and tariffs, the economies of North America became better integrated.

In 2018, the countries renegotiated their trade agreement to address concerns about intellectual property, unfair trade practices, and low wages. North American cars are preferred over those being imported from abroad, Canadians can import more duty-free goods from the US, and Mexico must legally protect the rights of workers in collective bargaining. Additionally, businesses can now operate from their own country, eliminating any need for subsidiary companies in the other countries. Together, with other changes, USMCA seeks to improve trade in North America.

How it is used: American dairy farmers can export more of their products to Canada under **USMCA**.

World Bank

international financial institution that provides loans to developing countries

What it is: a United Nations agency responsible for providing zero- or low-interest loans to lower- and middle-income countries trying to develop their physical capital

How it works: Low-income or middle-income countries, where the average household income is much smaller than the average American household's income, often lack significant savings to invest in physical capital (factories, roads, bridges, water systems, waste treatment systems, telecommunications systems, power plants, and electrical grids). This inability to invest keeps countries in a state of poverty. The World Bank was created after World War II to help lower-income countries by providing them grants and low-interest loans so they could begin to develop their capital and get out of poverty. The World Bank receives most of its funding from G7 countries.

How it is used: India borrowed from the **World Bank** so it could improve its electrical system.

WTO (World Trade Organization)

institution created to reduce tariffs and improve trade between nations

What it is: an organization that gathers representatives from various nations to negotiate freer trade by reducing trade barriers

How it works: Economists generally agree that free trade is beneficial to everyone because it improves the average standard of living. Every 2 years, heads of state and representatives from countries worldwide meet to discuss world trade and address issues which affect the ability of countries to trade freely with each other. Headquartered in Geneva, Switzerland, the WTO is the successor organization to the General Agreement on Tariffs and Trade, or GATT. GATT was created after World War II to address the many barriers to trade that sparked much of the conflicts in the nineteenth and early twentieth century. These organizations promote dialogue so international conflict over trade isn't as common.

How it is used: Many of the concerns about pollution and climate change become sticking points during **WTO** negotiations.

CHAPTER 10

Growth and Inequality

In this final chapter, we'll look at the words describing economic growth and inequality. Economic growth is seen when standards of living increase over time. Economists seek to understand what causes economic growth and develop theories and models to describe the source of growth, coming up with new terms. Although generally economic growth is a good thing, it is not without criticism. Economic growth is often uneven, leading to financial inequality. Economists identify factors that result in inequality; they use equations and models to better understand and describe it. From *capital deepening* to *inequality*, and *Lorenz curve* to *regressive tax*, these terms demonstrate how the economy works.

capital deepening

increases in buildings, machines, and tools per worker over time

What it is: if the rate at which capital accumulates in an economy over time is greater than the rate at which the labor force grows

How it works: When workers have access to capital, they can produce goods and services for the economy. The more capital that is available, the more the workers can produce. Capital deepening is the result of savings and investment. When people save money, businesses can use it to invest in new capital. This capital when combined with labor ultimately allows businesses to produce more goods and services. As the amount of capital per worker increases, so does the availability of goods and services in the economy.

How it is used: Increases in the number of tools and machines available to workers resulted in **capital deepening**.

capital formation

creation of new buildings, tools, machines, infrastructure, and equipment

What it is: businesses invest people's savings, resulting in increases in physical capital

How it works: Whenever businesses invest in new capital, the existing stock of capital increases. This process of capital formation is an important factor in determining the growth of an economy. If capital formation is greater than capital's eventual wear and tear (depreciation), the economy's capacity to grow increases. However, if capital formation does not keep up with depreciation, then the economy can't grow as quickly. Sufficient savings and relatively low interest rates encourage firms to borrow and invest in capital. Governments use tax incentives to encourage capital formation by taxing investment income at lower rates than wage income.

How it is used: As savings flow out of a country, the resulting higher interest rates discourage **capital formation**.

capital gains tax

tax on investment profits

What it is: a tax on income earned from selling real or financial assets at a price higher than their purchase price

How it works: When savers and investors purchase financial assets like shares of stock, bonds, or real assets like land and buildings, they can earn income in the forms of dividends, interest, or rent. However, they can also get income from capital gains—selling the asset for more than what they paid for it. Governments can choose to treat income from capital gains the same as income earned from other sources (like a job or interest on savings), or they can tax capital gains at a lower rate to encourage people and businesses to invest, resulting in economic growth. Favorable capital gains taxes are a source of intense political debate because they are seen as favoring the wealthy.

How it is used: Because of concerns over income inequality, Congress debated raising the **capital gains tax**.

economic growth

increase in an economy's output over time

What it is: the gradual increase in real GDP (gross domestic product) or in real GDP per capita

How it works: Economists measure an economy's economic growth by calculating changes in inflation-adjusted GDP over time. As a country's economy grows, more goods and services are produced every year.

Economic growth is usually expressed in terms of a growth rate. For example, the US economy grew at an annual rate of 3% in the second quarter of 2024. By measuring growth as a change in real GDP per capita rather than real GDP, economists have a better idea of how the average person's standard of living is changing over time. Factors influencing economic growth include increases in a country's savings, investment, physical capital and human capital, and increases in average labor productivity.

How it is used: Countries like those in Western Europe, China, and Japan face challenges to **economic growth** as their populations age and decline.

endogenous growth theory

innovation and economic growth result from more people having more ideas

What it is: changes in technology are internal results of people and firms innovating in response to incentives present in the economy

How it works: Economic growth is ultimately a result of increases in labor productivity and people's innovation increasing, resulting in creative advances in technology. So as the population grows, the capacity for the economy to grow increases as well because more people means more ideas. Differences in human capital in countries results in different growth rates. Governments play a key role in economic growth by directly funding or providing tax credits for research and development.

How it is used: Because India's population is growing at a faster rate than Japan's, **endogenous growth theory** predicts greater economic growth for India.

estate tax

tax on inheritance

What it is: the tax paid on the value of an inherited estate that's worth over a government-defined limit

How it works: When a person dies, they often leave behind assets like money, stocks, bonds, houses, and land. The value of these assets is subject to a tax if it exceeds a certain amount determined by law. Estate taxes are popular among economists because they raise revenue for the government and don't affect people's productivity or place a burden on lower-income households. In the US, the estate tax is levied on estates worth about $13 million for an individual or about $25 million for a couple, but these limits can vary from year to year.

How it is used: People can avoid **estate taxes** by setting up a trust for their assets.

exogenous growth theory

capital deepening results in economic growth

What it is: economic growth comes from increases in physical capital and external changes in technology

How it works: As more physical capital becomes available for workers, their productivity increases, resulting in economic growth. Technological changes and innovations are external to the model and improve the quality of an economy's physical capital, which further improves productivity. Differences in the amount of capital available per worker explain the differences in growth rates among countries. Government plays a key role in economic growth by providing tax credits to promote capital investment.

How it is used: Policymakers look to the **exogenous growth theory** as a rationale for providing investment tax credits to businesses.

flat tax

taxing everyone's income at the same rate

What it is: the government collects the same percentage of income from all taxpayers

How it works: A flat tax takes the same proportion of everyone's income in an economy. For example, if government levies a 15% flat tax, then every taxpayer owes 15% of their income to the government. An earner making $20,000 would owe $3,000 while an earner making $200,000 would owe $30,000. Although seemingly fair, flat taxes place a larger burden on lower-income households than households with higher incomes. Lower-income households spend a greater proportion of their income on necessities (not luxuries), so the tax will affect their ability to purchase the goods and services they need.

How it is used: A man running for political office promised to get rid of our complicated tax system and replace it with a simple **flat tax** of 15%.

GDP (gross domestic product) per capita

average income per person in an economy

What it is: the value of a country's output divided by the country's population

How it works: Economists use GDP per capita to measure the average income for an economy. The higher the number, the better off people in the economy are. Economists measure economic growth by monitoring changes in GDP per capita over time. By focusing on GDP per capita rather than GDP, economists can more clearly see how an economy's average person is faring. At current exchange rates, US GDP per capita was about $85,370 in 2024.

How it is used: If a country produces $1 billion in output with a population of 100,000, then its **GDP per capita** is $1 billion ÷ 100,000 people, or $10,000 per person.

gift tax

tax on transfers of money from one person to another

What it is: government taxes on transfers of money from one person to another if the transfer exceeds a certain amount

How it works: In 2024, a person in the US can gift $18,000 to someone else without paying a gift tax. So, a generous grandmother could give each of her children and grandchildren $18,000 without paying taxes. Any amount over the $18,000-per-person gift is subject to the gift tax. People with substantial assets often start reducing the size of their estates as they grow older to minimize any estate taxes owed, so the government places a gift tax to capture some of that wealth.

How it is used: Jill's grandfather gave her $20,000 and had to pay a **gift tax** on the $2,000 that was over the limit.

Gini coefficient

measure of income inequality

What it is: a calculation economists use to measure how income is distributed in an economy

How it works: Italian statistician Corrado Gini calculated income inequality by taking the area underneath a line of equality but above a Lorenz curve and comparing it to the total area under the line of equality. Gini coefficients range from 0, or perfect income equality, to 1, or perfect income inequality. If the Gini coefficient is closer to zero than one, then income is more evenly distributed among its population. However, as it approaches one, income in the economy is concentrated in only a few of the people. Countries with Gini coefficients of 0.3 and lower are viewed by economists as having a relatively high level of income equality.

How it is used: According to World Bank, the **Gini coefficient** for the US in 2022 was 0.413 and had increased significantly since 1980; however, the **Gini coefficient** of South Africa was 0.63.

human capital

people's mental and physical assets

What it is: the general health, knowledge, skills, and effort of individuals or the population in an economy

How it works: Human capital, or capability to work in an economy, is developed by having proper nutrition, housing, education, training, and incentives to produce. Governments can improve human capital by ensuring everyone has their basic needs met and by fostering an economic system that encourages people to produce, allowing them to have what they need and want. Measuring human capital is a challenge, so economists rely on real GDP per capita and the Human Development Index to get an idea of a country's human capital.

How it is used: Although the developing world lacks adequate physical capital, its **human capital** is a source of economic growth and opportunity.

income redistribution

taxing people with higher incomes and transferring the money to people with lower or no income

What it is: the government effort to ensure households with lower or no income receive some type of income funded by taxpayers with higher incomes

How it works: Government collects taxes on household incomes through the federal income tax and the Social Security tax. These tax revenues are then spent on the government's budget, part of which is payments to low- or no-income households. For example, Social Security taxes are collected from working-age people's incomes and redistributed to people with disabilities and retirees because they may otherwise lack sufficient income to support their consumption of goods and services. Income redistribution also comes in the form of government subsidies to businesses paid for by taxpayers.

How it is used: Income redistribution results in taxpayers bearing the cost of supporting some of the jobless people in an economy.

inequality

income and wealth are not evenly distributed in an economy

What it is: households have differing levels of wealth and income in an economy

How it works: Income inequality means that some households have larger incomes than others. Wealth inequality means that some households have more wealth than others. Government addresses inequality through income redistribution and taxes those with higher incomes and wealth through income taxes, property taxes, and estate taxes.

Income inequality is primarily the result of differences in human capital (education, training, and necessities and wants met) among individuals and their level of productivity; those with more human capital and productivity tend to earn more than those without. Wealth inequality may result from productivity but also from generational wealth being transferred within families.

How it is used: Inequality is a source of economic and political conflict in market-based societies.

investment tax credit

government policy that encourages businesses to invest in capital

What it is: payments to businesses who then invest in buildings, machines, and equipment

How it works: To encourage economic growth and development in certain industries or areas of the country, the government sometimes offers investment tax credits to businesses. The businesses receive these tax credits for investing in specific capital or by expanding their businesses. For example, many businesses receive investment tax credits from the government for investing in solar power to reduce reliance on greenhouse gases. Also, local governments may offer investment tax credits to encourage business expansion in underserved communities.

How it is used: A local business received an **investment tax credit** for installing solar panels on the roof of their building.

labor productivity

economic output of the workforce per hour worked

What it is: the amount of output produced by the workforce in an hour given some existing amount of physical capital

How it works: Labor productivity depends on the amount of human capital and physical capital available. As the amount of human and physical capital increases, labor productivity increases. Increases in labor productivity result in economic growth. For example, during periods of recession, it's common for the existing workforce's labor productivity to increase. This is because their human capital increases with experience and more physical capital is available per worker because of higher levels of unemployment.

How it is used: The economy was able to produce more output this year than last year with the same number of workers and the same amount of physical capital because **labor productivity** increased.

Laffer curve

raising tax rates eventually reduces tax revenue

What it is: the relationship between the tax rate and tax revenue is initially positive, but then ultimately raising tax rates further reduces tax revenue

How it works: Economist Arthur Laffer theorized that at some unknown tax rate, increasing it will result in the government collecting less tax revenue. For example, increasing the tax rate on income from 0% to 10% will increase revenue to the government, and increasing the tax rate from 10% to 30% may increase revenue even further. However, increasing the tax rate from 30% to 100% will reduce the amount of tax collected because people will no longer have an incentive to work.

How it is used: The **Laffer curve** gained notoriety during the 1980 presidential election, when Ronald Reagan argued for reducing income tax rates in the US; ultimately tax revenue decreased rather than increased relative to the size of the government's budget.

Lorenz curve

economic model showing the level of income inequality in a country

What it is: a model that shows the distribution of income among households in an economy

How it works: By comparing the percentage of income being earned by a percentage of households, the Lorenz curve maps out a country's income distribution. The Lorenz curve is shown with a line of equality. The line of equality represents perfectly equal distribution of income in the economy. The closer the Lorenz curve approximates the line of equality, the more the level of income inequality diminishes. The greater the level of income inequality, the more the Lorenz curve dips away from the line of equality.

How it is used: The area between the **Lorenz curve** and the line of equality is smaller for countries with more even income distributions.

microfinance

making small loans to help reduce poverty

What it is: small loans made to help entrepreneurs in low-income areas, which then helps to reduce poverty

How it works: People (usually women) in low-income countries without access to traditional sources of credit can borrow money from a microfinance institution. This way, they can invest in the capital necessary to start or expand a small business. For example, many people in South Asia and sub-Saharan Africa do not have access to traditional finance, making it difficult for would-be entrepreneurs. Microfinance institutions specialize in making small loans to individuals so they can purchase things like sewing machines, livestock, or simple tools.

How it is used: The online **microfinance** platform Kiva allows people to make small loans to entrepreneurs in developing countries.

progressive tax

government charges tax rates directly based on income

What it is: a tax that takes a larger percentage of income from people with high incomes than from people with lower incomes

How it works: Progressive taxes, like the US federal income tax, take a larger share of income from higher-income earners than from lower-income earners. For example, assume one person earns $40,000 while another person earns $400,000. Then, assume that they are both single and have no dependents. If the marginal tax rates are 0% on the first $30,000 of income, 15% on the next $70,000 of income, and 25% on all income greater than $100,000, then the $40,000 income earner would pay ($40,000 – $30,000) × 15% or $1,500 in taxes, which is ($1,500 ÷ $40,000) × 100 or 3.75% of their income in taxes. Assuming the same marginal tax rates, the $400,000 income earner would pay (15% × $70,000) + (25% × $300,000) or $85,500 in taxes, which is ($85,500 ÷ $400,000) × 100 or 21.38% of their income in taxes.

How it is used: Countries with **progressive taxes** tend to have lower levels of income inequality.

regressive tax

tax where lower-income people pay more as a share of their income

What it is: a tax that places a larger burden on people with lower incomes than on people with higher incomes

How it works: Taxes are regressive when people with lower incomes end up paying a larger share of their income in the tax than do people with higher incomes. For example, sales taxes are typically regressive. Assume a person with a $40,000 income and a person with a $400,000 income both buy a sandwich. If the sandwich cost $8.00 and the sales tax rate is 6%, then the total paid for the sandwich will be $8.48. The $0.48 in tax represents a larger share of the $40,000 income than it does of the $400,000 income.

How it is used: States that do not have an income tax often raise revenue through sales taxes, which are a **regressive tax** because people with less income pay a larger portion of their income in sales tax than do people with more income.

supply-side economics

economic policy focused on increasing saving, investment, and productivity

What it is: government policies to increase the economy's LRAS (long-run aggregate supply)

How it works: Removing government regulations and restrictions from businesses, using policies like investment tax credits, reducing taxes on interest income and capital gains, or directly funding research and development are all examples of supply-side economics. Most economic policy in the latter half of the twentieth century focused on boosting aggregate demand in the economy, but supply-side economics emerged in the 1980s as a response. By pursuing economic growth as the primary goal of policy rather than economic stability, supply-side economists argue that you get both growth and stability.

How it is used: Supply-side economics is popular among political conservatives because it calls for a reduction in government involvement in the economy through deregulation.

tax incidence

markets determine whether consumers, producers, or both bear the burden of a tax

What it is: ultimately who pays the burden of a tax depends on the market

How it works: Although government may tax a producer by law, that tax burden may be transferred to the consumer if the producer can pass the full value of the tax onto them. For example, assume the government places a $0.50 tax per gallon on gasoline to be paid by producers. If producers can effectively charge $0.50 per gallon more to consumers, then the burden of the tax (tax incidence) falls either completely or partially on the consumer, even though the government means to tax the producer.

How it is used: Economists look at the effects of taxes on the supply and demand for a product to determine the **tax incidence**.

Index

The finance book you wish you'd had in school.

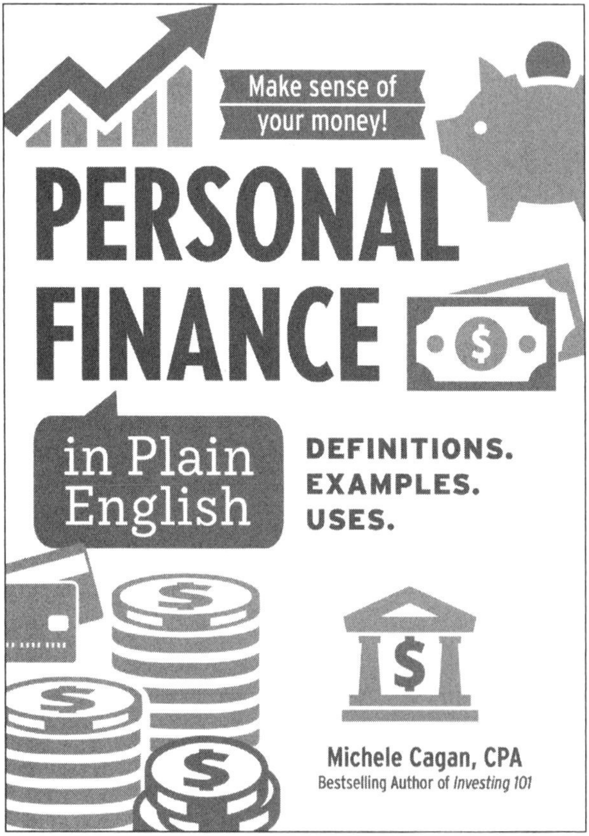